MOON
PHASES

Andrews McMeel Publishing
a division of Andrews McMeel Universal
1130 Walnut Street, Kansas City, Missouri 64106

www.andrewsmcmeel.com

VividaTM is a trademark property of White Star s.r.l.
www.vividabooks.com

© Originally published in 2021 by White Star s.r.l.
Piazzale Luigi Cadorna, 6
20123 Milano, Italia
www.whitestar.it

22 23 24 25 26 RLP 10 9 8 7 6 5 4 3 2 1

ISBN: 978-1-5248-7180-2

Library of Congress Control Number: 2021949224

Editor: Katie Gould
Production Editor: Thea Voutiritsas
Production Manager: Tamara Haus

ATTENTION: SCHOOLS AND BUSINESSES
Andrews McMeel books are available at quantity discounts with bulk purchase for educational, business, or sales promotional use. For information, please e-mail the Andrews McMeel Publishing Special Sales Department: specialsales@amuniversal.com.

CECILIA LATTARI

MOON PHASES

Use the lunar cycle to connect with nature and focus your intentions

Illustrated by Emilio Ignozza

Andrews McMeel
PUBLISHING®

Index

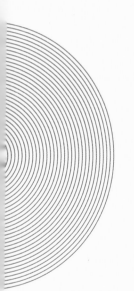

For Ginevra, who will soon learn how to read.

For Rahela and Angela, who know that books can carry you far away.

Introduction

When I was a child and I was riding in the car with my parents in the evening, I imagined that I had a string in my hand that tied me to the moon. She was my own personal balloon, high up in the air, round and shining. I kept my little fist closed tightly so that the string that took me to her could not get away.

I never let go of that string as I was growing up; and when I went back to live in a small mountain town, I thought, "Ah, I can finally celebrate the Full Moon, gazing at it through the trees." The moon has been my confidante many times; she has listened when I tell her of my joy and pain and ask her advice as I bask in her light.

The moon undeniably has magic of its own. As well as having inspired poets, writers, directors, and artists of all kinds, it has been a point of reference for almost every culture since ancient times. Planting seeds, pruning trees, and many other agricultural activities follow the moon's cycles, and there are books that suggest in which phase it is best to cut your hair, undergo an operation, harvest herbs, and so on.

Observing the moon and working with its phases is also of great use when it comes to self-care and growth. It helps us better understand our inner rhythms and connect to the rhythms of nature.

This book allows the reader to connect with the moon's varying energies as they change from month to month and phase to phase. The book narrates twelve moons, one for each month of the year, and a thirteenth moon, the Blue Moon.

My explanations of the symbols, messages, and practices associated with each moon are based on the days of the New Moon, or *Esbat* as they are called in pagan and neo-pagan traditions. The name *Esbat* comes from the old French word *ébat*, which means *celebration* or *small feast*. *Esbat* are days dedicated to the moon, in which the goddess is celebrated, are days of intimate expressions, when goals that have been achieved are celebrated, and future wishes are planned.

To explain the energies that move through the different months of the year, I began with the *Sabbat*, eight pagan and neo-pagan celebrations dedicated to specific moments in the year. The word *Sabbat* comes from the Italian word *sabba*, which means *feast* or *magical meeting*. The *Sabbat* are associated with the movements of the sun; they are days of power, inspiration, and celebration. They perfectly express the natural flow of time, the cycle of months and seasons, and of the earth's rhythms. The eight: Samhain, on October 31; Yule or winter solstice on December 21; Imbolc or Candlemas on February 2; Ostara or spring equinox on March 21; Beltane on May 1; Litha or summer solstice on June 21; Lughnasadh or Lammas on August 1; and Mabon or autumn equinox on September 21.

Each chapter is dedicated to a specific moon, which has many names. Most of the names that I have used are of European tradition, particularly Anglo-Saxon and Germanic, but some belong to Native American culture. There are other names for a moon according to the month it falls in; often they reflect the events that take place in that specific moment of the year and in a specific part of the world. The names I chose come prevalently from European tradition; I feel they are more suitable for the influences and energies that I have used to explore and come to know the lunar messages. I have selected the most evocative ones, the ones that best describe each month's moon.

I took into consideration the four phases of every moon, each of which expresses a particular feeling:

NEW MOON – The period of the New Moon occurs when the part of the moon facing the earth is completely shaded, when the moon is between the earth and the sun. For this reason, the New Moon always occurs in the same zodiac sign as the sun. The energies of the New Moon are restorative, fresh, and primitive, and they lead to the creation of new, original projects that can grow and mature. Organization is favored, and in these days you may feel the need for solitude and the desire to withdraw from the world around you in order to dedicate yourself to new projects.

WAXING MOON – The phase immediately following the New Moon is the Waxing Moon, a small shining crescent full of potential. The moon grows for fourteen days. The first seven days trace its growth from New Moon to Half Moon and the other seven from Half Moon to Full Moon. In the first seven days, the moon is called First Quarter; in the last seven, Waxing Gibbous. In this phase, the energies are ones of welcoming, growth, and regeneration.

FULL MOON – When the moon is Full and the side that faces the earth is opposite the sun, for two or three days, it looks like a shining sphere in the sky. During this phase, its energies are at their height; it is a delicate passage that can be useful to define plans, reflect, and stay in touch with your intuition.

WANING MOON – Now the moon begins to wane, day after day; and after about fourteen days, it will be New again. From the third to the seventh day after the Full Moon, the moon is called the Waning Gibbous; from the seventh to the fourteenth, it is called the Last Quarter or Balsamic Moon. The energies in this phase are ones of release, cleansing, and completed manifestation.

In each chapter, the symbols associated with that specific moon are explained. They can be used to connect with the moon's energies, by decorating your home, and by choosing the right clothing, colors, objects, etc. In addition, for each moon I suggest a number of practices and rituals. These will help you use the influence of the energies present in that moment to bring magic into your daily life.

Every moon has an associated planet with popular history references, herbal uses, and its own message spoken in its own soft voice. Lastly, I have associated some of the moons with famous celebrities, veritable pop icons whose nature and art can help reveal the lunar message.

I believe the moon is not that far away, that it accompanies us on our journey, reminding us to observe closely the magic that surrounds us. She is actually very close to all of us.

The Wolf Moon

Also known as
Calm Moon, Ice Moon,
Small Winter Moon,
Chaste Moon,
and Bright Moon.

It is a powerful moon
with a clear, sharp voice
that can be stern at times.

J anuary is the peak of winter, a month of retreat when everything is sleeping; a time to draw close together, in your own home, in contact with your own tribe, as wolves do.

In fact, the wolf is the inspiration of this January moon; a moon that is wild and solitary but that also knows the importance of unity and carries in it a sense of belonging. Your tribe is not necessarily the family into which you were born; it is all the people you feel akin to, that you care about, those who are your friends and who make up your chosen team. The emotional context of this family is well expressed by a word that has become very widely used: *Hygge.* This Danish and Norwegian word describes the sense of well-being and joy that we feel when we are in a familiar place, comfortable, and surrounded by friends, enjoying life's small daily pleasures.

January is the first month of the year, the month when we make resolutions, when all things have yet to be written, but it is also the bitterest month, when nature is dormant; rapt, reflecting on what will be, sleeping, and waiting in the womb. It is the moment of Capricorn, an earth sign that is minimal, lucid, and prone to pragmatism. When the sun is in Capricorn, the Full Moon is in the opposing sign, Cancer, meaning that at times, feelings get the better of reason. January's moon may make you feel like spending all afternoon under the covers, reading and dreaming on one hand and like having dinner under soft lights, surrounded by the chatter of your closest friends on the other. There is nothing strange about feeling like a lone wolf and needing your wonderful, unique pack at the same time.

From an emotional and mindful point of view, the month of January is a journey in which you simultaneously feel the need for solitude and inner searching and an urge to surround yourself with loved ones. This moon's voice will advise you to leave some empty space inside you and to cleanse in order to welcome the new.

Lunar Phases

WITH THE NEW MOON in January, you can dedicate yourself to activities that will improve your work: make a business plan, organize projects for the new year or at least for the next three months, take a day entirely for yourself to reflect about how to develop something original, whether it be related to your job or your personal growth. This can be the ideal time to abandon something you really want to remove from your life: kick the cigarette habit, start a vegetarian or vegan diet, cut the dead branches from your relationships, and focus your attention on the things that make you productive. January's New Moon tells you: "To receive, you must first create space."

DURING THE WAXING MOON in January, in accordance with the energies of the month, you can connect with your desire for renewal. This tendency appears in this moment, precisely because we are at the beginning of the new year. Use this lunar phase to connect, to see the people you love, to open the doors in your home, to organize dinners with close friends, and to reawaken that quality of the wolf that makes you take care of your special extended family.

WITH THE FULL MOON in January, you can develop your intuition: reflect about your family and your ancestors, rediscover their history, and listen to those who make up your community. Planning is important during this Full Moon. Observe the results you have obtained and balance your goals. You can dedicate these days to studying and a more in-depth examination of a subject that interests you and that develops your intellect.

DURING THE WANING MOON in January, you can listen to your friends as you prepare a cup of tea, you can be receptive as you consciously listen, and you can let go of what you no longer need. For example, by selecting clothes that you do not use and donating them to those who need them. Look at things as they really are and ask yourself: Is it worth it? Do I really need it? What are my necessities?

Plant

The mountain ash is a beautiful tree that can grow as tall as 16½ yards (15 meters). As a child, I was attracted to its small red berries that looked to me like the apples of fairies; and with a child's intuition, I had seen right. Also known as the service tree or sorb tree, it is considered magical by the Celts. They dedicated a significant period of the year to it, from January 21 to February 15, after the winter solstice when the light begins to triumph over the dark.

They planted this magical tree in front of their houses to ward off storms and lightning strikes. In ancient Ireland, warriors used the wood of the tree to propitiate the gods in their battles, casting spells on fires made of its wood, and asking the warrior spirits to fight by their sides.

The fruit of the tree is dried or cooked for use in phytotherapy; it can be toxic if ingested fresh or uncooked, a problem that can be avoided by cooking the fruit into jam or syrup, both of which have astringent properties. The buds of the *Sorbus domestica* are useful in gemmotherapy for their vasoregulatory properties.

Symbolically, the tree, which was sacred to the goddess Brigid (associated with fertility in Celtic mythology), is linked to inspiration, poetry, and fire. The Celtic name of the tree, *Luis*, means "flame": a flame that heightens your senses and improves your sight, allowing you to see more clearly without masking reality.

The mountain ash tells you, "Be unconventional and do not be afraid to see things with your own eyes."

Mountain Ash

Sorbus domestica L. or Sorbus aucuparia L.

I

15

Symbols

WOLF

The primary symbol of this moon represents the ability to teach, individuality, the capacity to give shape, group awareness, loyalty, devotion, talent, focus on detail, security, and family.

SNOWDROP AND CROCUS

The flowers associated with this moon represent the beauty in difficulty, rebirth, and clear intuition.

GRAY, VIOLET, AND WHITE

The colors associated with this moon are linked to the cold, to rest, to purity, and to intuition.

CRONE

The feminine side associated with this moon is the old, wise woman, the crone, the one who knows and holds the secret of time. She waits and knows when the time is right, like the winter, quiet and seemingly immobile. A momentary pause while life prepares for its rebirth.

THE HERMIT

The Hermit is the Tarot card that represents introspection, the ability to live in solitude as a resource, and self-knowledge.

TIGER'S-EYE OR CAT'S-EYE

Both are particular stones that become opalescent under the light, revealing what looks like an eye in their veining. They are used to acquire a clear, precise vision and to make the right decisions.

MOUNTAIN ASH FRUIT OR APPLES

One of the reasons these fruits symbolize this moon is the star-shaped formation of seeds, which appear when an apple is cut horizontally, or on the bottom of mountain-ash berries.

Practices and Rituals

Begin to keep a *lunar journal* where you will write down your projects, dreams, and wishes. Use as many images as you can, but keep in mind, it is not intended to be a board on Pinterest (although you could make one of those also). Choose images and photos that you like from magazines, brochures, and inspiration pages. Cut them out and make your collage of wishes.

Choose an afternoon to invite your best friends for a cup of tea and make them *Wolf Moon cookies*. You will need 1 cup (200 g) of flour, a packet of yeast for sweets, 8 ounces (225 g) of margarine or butter, 1½ cups (375 g) of raw sugar, an egg, and a teaspoon of vanilla extract. Use these ingredients to make shortbread dough, let it rest for half an hour in the refrigerator, roll it out, and cut out half-moon-shaped cookies. Bake them in a 350°F (180°C) oven for about ten minutes.

Make a necklace out of mountain-ash berries, stringing them on a red thread with a needle. You can wear it as a personal amulet to ward off trouble. You can gather the berries from the ash tree yourself, or you can buy them in an herbalist shop or online.

Get yourself a deck of Tarot cards if you do not already have one, and reflect on the message of the Hermit.

Bathe in the light of the Full Moon, in your yard, in a park, or in the woods, and let its rays illuminate you. You can dress in white or in comfortable clothes made of natural fibers. Take a soft shawl to protect yourself from the January cold.

If you do not feel like going out, observe the moon from indoors and invent your own Wolf Dance, remembering to howl often.

Björk

Track: "It's Oh So Quiet" (from the album *Post*, 1995)

Pop Icon

If we follow the solitary nature of the Wolf Moon, we might meet Björk. She was born in Iceland, the land of ice and fire. Her style is original and unique, and her music covers a number of genres. Her productions, music videos, and stage outfits are unique, extravagant, and lunar. Björk always finds a balance between technology and music and accompanies her live events with outlandish performances and displays.

Just like the moon in January, her style tells us, "You can do this!" You can be one of the "strange" ones and still achieve what you envision, your own imaginary world, in reality. Allow yourself to dress exactly as you want to, even if it is not always simple, because your style, the clothes and accessories you choose and the colors, are part of your personality and the message you want to convey. Do not be afraid to wear something that others see as eccentric; use it as your stage costume. Remember to make it fun when you open your wardrobe.

Embrace your introverted side; the Wolf Moon brings reflection and inner dialogue. Björk may be shy and reserved, but at the same time, she is a rock star! So if you need time for yourself, take it, even if it is only for fifteen minutes. If you need to make a phone call, but you do not want to, send a voice message or an e-mail. Find the time to read, to gaze out the window. Sink into the water in the bathtub, surrounded by a colonnade of scented candles, or give yourself the opportunity to simply stay in silence, to observe, and meditate.

A view that is both clear and vast makes it possible to bring together ideas that seem far apart but that have something to say to one another, a common voice, like a red thread. "Dare without fear," whispers the wolf that inhabits this moon.

I

21

The Snow Moon

Also known as
Ice Moon and Wild Moon.

The moon in February comes
in a time of promises, in which
we must believe in reawakening
even though there are still no
evident signs of life.

The Snow Moon is the perfect name for the moon in February, because in this period we are still, just like seeds beneath a blanket of snow. At the same time, we are beginning to feel the air around us change; February carries the seed of the spring that is coming. It combines both rest and activity, the silence and the crackle of wood in the fireplace.

We are still in winter, but the warm rays of the sun, a different light, and the dew sparkling on the bare tree limbs can catch us by surprise in February. Everything is still, but everything is about to move, exactly like the snow that falls, making the landscape magical for a moment, and then melts just as quickly, revealing the soft earth below it with newly sprouting grass and the fragrance of spring, or almost. If we touch the ground, we will feel that it is warmer and that it is beginning to awaken under the snow.

The word *February* comes from the Latin word *februare*, which means "to purify"; the energy in this period is primarily associated with purification, renewal, cleansing, clearing space, and renovation. This is also the time of Candlemas, which originated as a Celtic celebration of the rebirth of the light and the pagan feast Imbolc, which literally means "in the womb." Imbolc was dedicated to the goddess Brigid, associated with the fruits of the earth and the sacred fire of creativity.

I like to point out that two complementary forces move in the month of February. On one hand, there is the need to stay, to wait, and remain in the womb; and on the other, the need to purify, give new life, and make space, and if you think about it, everything that is born needs rest and time as well as movement and growth. You can dedicate your time in February to the activities and practices that use both of these forces, like the flame of a candle that slowly lights the room with the liberating, cleansing power of its brilliance.

Lunar Phases

WITH THE NEW MOON in February, you can dedicate some time to understanding what you want to keep and what you want to eliminate. Make a list of the things in your house, your clothes, your personal care products, and even the food in your pantry, then set aside everything that is broken, unrepairable, worn out, or that you have not used in over a year. Divide it into bags and decide which things you can donate and which things you have no choice but to throw away!

DURING THE WAXING MOON in February, take a moment to analyze your projects (the ones you made a business plan for in January, for example) in order to understand where they stand, what they need to continue their progress, and how long their incubation period will last. What can you do now and in the coming month about your plans? This is the right time to nourish the seeds of your wishes with attention, care, and planning.

WITH THE FULL MOON in February, devote yourself to a ritual of beauty and care just for you—a scented bath, an evening of reading by candlelight, or simply a moment of daydreaming, as you relax. Welcome the opportunity to do nothing and celebrate this instant while the moon is at its apex. Let its rays of snow caress you and make you feel you are truly safe, just like a seed under the snow, almost ready to sprout.

DURING THE WANING MOON in February, take stock of your candleholders and take the time to clean them, removing waxy residue and throwing away candles that are old or ruined, or that have been lit and put out many times. Renew your incense corner and light incense or dried herbs to cleanse your house of stagnant energy. Open the windows and let the fresh air in for a few minutes every day.

Plant

I n its study of the sage plant, the ancient Schola Medica Salernitana (Salernitana School of Medicine) posed the question, "Why should a man who has a garden with sage in it die?" In fact, the sage plant has so many beneficial properties that it is impossible to get sick if you are lucky enough to own one.

You can recognize sage by its velvety leaves and fragrance, which is reminiscent of your grandmother's roasted potatoes at Sunday dinner or the herbal tea you drink with a splash of lemon juice. This Mediterranean plant is perennial and evergreen. It is part woody and part leafy and the hue of its leaves is so particular that a color has been named for it: *sage green.*

It is a symbol of health, the word from which its name derives—*salus* or the adjective *salvus*—and is associated with the protection of the home and those who live there. It is one of the herbs most commonly used in smudge sticks, bundles of dried herbs tied together and burned like incense to purify the home.

Sage is astringent, disinfectant, and anti-inflammatory. It is used together with bay leaves in digestive herbal teas and is an efficient cough suppressant when served as an herbal tea with honey added. It is also effective in treating inflammation of the oral cavity, gingivitis, and irritations. The phytoestrogen contained in sage can help regulate the menstrual cycle.

At one time it was tradition to plant a sage plant when a baby was born, so that the plant and the human could grow together. Sage is thought to offer protection from nightmares and unpleasant visions.

Its message is: "Clear your path and have the courage to let go."

Sage

Salvia officinalis

II

27

Symbols

SNOW

Snow is the quintessential symbol of this moon. Snow is enchantment, the silence in that moment before everything begins to happen. It is the breath before spring and the symbol of purity and light.

WHITE

The color associated with this time of year is white, both for its allusion to snow and for its symbology, which includes purification and open space, like that of a new, blank page, waiting to be written on.

ASH

For the Celts, this month is dedicated to the ash tree, a symbol of wisdom and healing. The mythological giant ash, *Yggdrasill*, the tree where Odin hung himself, is considered a cosmic tree.

BARLEY

Barley is a nutritious grain that is sweet and soft, and when it is ground it produces a white milky substance, which is why it is often associated with the month of February and this moon. Barley chaff is used to make soft cushions that are ideal for relaxation and rejuvenating sleep.

THE STAR

The Tarot card associated with this moon is the Star; it is the hope, the seed that lays dormant, and the trust in luck, the future, and the first ray of sun.

CANDLES

Candles, a characteristic symbol of the month of February, are blessed during Candlemas and can be found in all the celebrations of the return of the light, of the purification by fire, of inner warmth, and the flame of Brigid that burns in the heart of artists.

Practices and Rituals

Gather all the new candles you have in the house and then buy more to use in the coming months. During the night of the Full Moon, expose them to the lunar light to infuse them with the moon's magic. If you like, in the morning you can rub them with lavender-scented oil and wrap them in a clean cloth.

To prepare a scrub dedicated to the goddess Brigid, you will need two cups of barley meal (or oatmeal), two spoons of rose petals or dried lavender flowers, two spoons of sweet almond oil, and two spoons of white clay powder (if you can find it; otherwise, you can make your scrub without it). Stir the ingredients together, then mix them in a blender. To use your scrub, mix a small amount with lukewarm water and massage it into your face.

If you are lucky enough to live where the snow is clean, go outside and get a cup of it. Mix it with a cup of olive oil to make *snow oil* to use on burns and skin irritations.

Before going to bed, make yourself a cup of oat or rice milk with a lot of honey, cinnamon, and a pinch of saffron. It is a fantastic sleep aid and a special treat.

Fill one room of the house with candles, light them one by one, and go close to the flame to feel its heat. Then light one in the center of the room, sit down near it, and cup its flame with your hands. When you are ready, put your hands on the ground and transmit the heat; envision the earth itself as it reawakens, with grass that grows green as spring arrives.

Buy tulip bulbs and plant them in a pot. They will bloom in the spring.

Put coarse salt in the corners of your rooms and on your doorstep for protection.

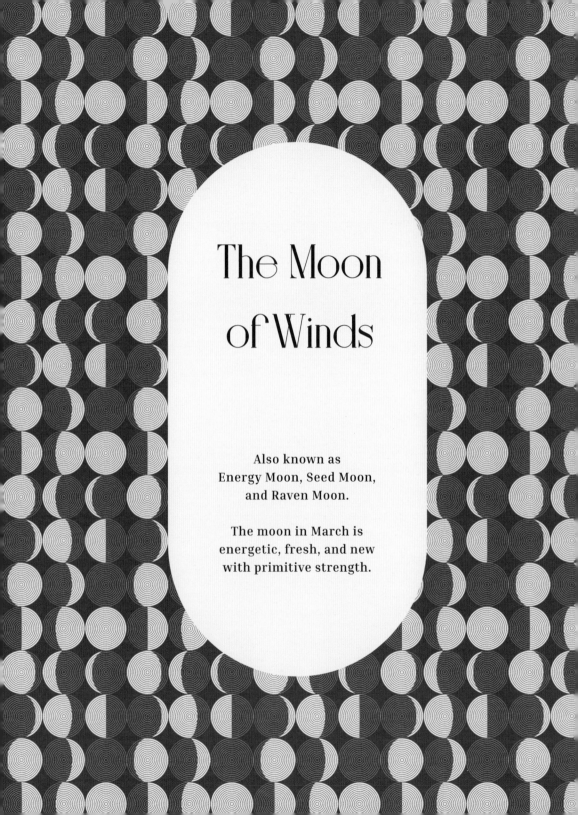

The Moon of Winds

Also known as
Energy Moon, Seed Moon,
and Raven Moon.

The moon in March is
energetic, fresh, and new
with primitive strength.

T wo forces mix in March: it is not spring yet; winter is not over. Outside, the sun sweetly warms the earth, blades of grass turn light green, and buds and sprouts appear. The life that is reawakening is tempered by the dregs of winter, which is still producing storms, cold winds, and some mornings, frost on the fields. In March, under the influence of the Moon of Winds, two forces come together, rest and reawakening, a space in which one is created from the other. Spring is nothing but winter in transformation.

When the snow melts into water and seeps into the ground, making it soft and fertile, the seed is ready to sprout. The seed and bud may be fragile, but they possess the strength to break through the ground, to tear open the membrane that covers them, and to come to life. The same energy resides in the March moon, like the wind that changes in this season, from strong to mild, from a gale to an evening breeze, when you can smell spring in the air. You cannot see it yet, but it is there.

March is the month of Aries, aggressive and dynamic; and just like Mars, the planet that governs it, it carries a message of vitality and energy. This is a budding moon, like the young, fiery Aries and like the sap that begins to flow in plants again, the chlorophyll makes the leaves turn green and allows a vital exchange of energy to take place.

Potential can be seen in the energy of the buds on the tree branches, at the center of the bud, in the empty space that grows, takes shape, and becomes a leaf, a plant, and ultimately a complete tree. In phytotherapy, this is the time of year when bud extracts are prepared, so March is a pivotal month for harvesting and macerating the buds that are used to prepare the remedies that contain the full potential of the plant. Something similar happens to our heart when it reawakens in the spring; its pulse increases, it takes root in the warm sun, and it slowly unfolds and opens like a leaf.

Lunar Phases

WITH THE NEW MOON in March, you can begin to deep-clean your house. This month's spring-cleaning will bring the fresh energy and renewal of the March moon. Open your windows, throw away what you no longer use, and start to clean up your yard. The New Moon is the best time to take care of your flower beds, eliminate the dry parts of your plants, and prepare the ground for planting or transplanting. Dig your hands into the fresh soil of March and feel the message of life it brings.

DURING THE WAXING MOON in March, you can choose the seeds you want to plant in your yard or in pots on your terrace. The moment is right to focus on the ideas you want to put in place in the coming trimester. Dedicate your attention to your plants as though they were flower seeds that you love. What do they need in order to sprout? What resources do they have to face the last cold days of winter?

III

35

WITH THE FULL MOON in March, heed the new wind and make a talisman for it; attach seashells, bells, and feathers on a colored thread, about half an inch apart, and use a small piece of wood as a clasp. You can hang your talisman in the window and listen to the March wind as it sings. This small Full Moon ritual will heighten your sense of openness to new things, things to face, not with fear but with levity and playfulness. Let the coolness of the spring wind speak to you and your projects, and infuse them with life.

DURING THE WANING MOON in March, put yourself in the hands of the wind you listened to with the last moon. Let it take away your anxieties and relieve you of your troubles. Learn to let go and let it be. Every now and then, open your arms and let the air embrace you, lift you up, and remind you that you have wings. Keep in touch with the change that often arrives with the March wind. Begin a new life cycle. Abandon your baggage from the past when it gets heavy and useless. Entrust it to the wind.

Plant

Nettle is the plant that best expresses the vital message of the Moon of Winds. A simple plant, its most characteristic feature is that it stings. You will recognize it when you touch it, from the irritation it causes on your skin. It has microscopic hairs on the bottom of its leaves called *trichomes,* which break on contact, releasing formic acid, histamine, and acetylcholine. Nettles defend themselves and reveal themselves at the same time. When it shows itself to you by stinging you, the plant teaches you healthy boundaries and how to respect them and make others respect them, in your life, too.

The nettle plant is a little green warrior, associated with Mars, not only because of its love of iron (it grows in iron-rich soil and is a good indicator of iron levels) but also for its connection to blood. Its ability to enhance blood and stimulate the formation of ferritin make it a useful remedy for anemia. It is very rich in chlorophyll, iron, sulfur, and silica and is a beneficial addition to our diet.

In Hans Christian Andersen's fairy tale "The Wild Swans," Princess Elisa must use nettles to knit eleven tunics in order to free her brothers of a wicked spell that has turned them into swans. But she was unable to finish one of the tunics, so when the last of the brothers was turned back into a man, he had a wing instead of an arm. The voice of the nettles asks us to look at all people for what they are; in their diversity and uniqueness, each one is special.

The message of the nettle is: "Look attentively; each of us is unique." At first sight, it might appear to be a plant like any other, but look more closely, or touch it, and it will show you just how original it is. It urges you to ask yourself, "What unique feature do I see in others? What is invisible to me? What can I do to make my uniqueness a resource?"

Nettle

Urtica dioica

III

37

III

38

Symbols

SEED

The seed, one of this moon's most powerful symbols, is both strong and fragile; the vitality of a seed that sprouts and breaks through the earth, and the membrane that covers it, to begin transformation and a new life. A seed knows when to germinate. It may lie dormant for years and awaken only when conditions are favorable. The seed is the nucleus of every project and every construction that begins with one step that is both fragile and strong.

GREEN

The color associated with this moon is green: the light green of sprouts, the first blades of grass, and the buds on the trees; green like life that pulses, reawakens, and makes way.

THE EMPEROR

The Tarot card associated with this moon is the Emperor, sitting on his throne but ready to jump into action. He is protective and determines rightful confines. Similar to the nettle plant, the Emperor charts healthy boundaries that allow your own unique nature to bloom fully.

ARTEMIS

The goddess associated with the Moon of Winds is Artemis (or Diana), the goddess of the forests who governs the indomitable spirit of every woman. She protects the sisterhood, and her arrow is the symbol of the vital strength we dedicate to our projects, to determining who we are, to becoming who we are, and to our wild spirit.

VIOLETS AND PRIMROSES

The flowers that characterize this time of year are the first ones to peek out—the violet, who is a bit shyer, and the primrose, who is more extroverted. Both are ideal for decorating or flavoring dishes and drinks. They say that if you eat a primrose, you can see the fairies. You have to try it to believe it.

Practices and Rituals

Choose the seeds for your pots; marigolds, primroses, poppies, daisies, and many wildflowers are planted this season. Take a piece of recycled paper and write down the things you would like to accomplish in the coming months, in a few key words that sum up your plans. Bury your list when you plant your seeds, then take care of your plants in the months that follow.

Begin to sprout seeds at home. You can make a homemade seed sprouter using recycled containers or a glass jar. Buy seeds that will produce edible sprouts to add to your salads; as well as tasting good, they are very healthful.

Write a poem or a song to bless the seeds you will plant in your garden or on your terrace.

Light a light-green candle at home and diffuse the essential oils of lemon, sage, or melissa to cleanse the air of stagnant energy.

During spring cleaning, use a broom to sweep negative energy from your windows and doors; and while you do, envision a black fog lifting and rolling away. As you are sweeping, you can talk to the energy and tell it to go away.

Follow the nature of Aries and choose a project that you want to begin, or put new energy into an activity that you left temporarily. Dance, light incense, and invent songs and lullabies to nurture your sprouts.

Choose a hat that you like and decorate it with wildflowers, just as Anne of Green Gables did.

Add primroses, violets, and other edible fresh flowers to your beverages.

Remember to touch the ground, to breathe in the wind, and to let the sun of spring caress you.

Lucy Liu

Track: Luis Bacalov, "The Grand Duel (Parte Prima)"
(from the album *Kill Bill Vol. 1 Original Soundtrack*, 2003)

III

42

Pop Icon

Lucy Liu. Her name is enough to conjure images of a warrior, thanks to one of her most famous roles, that of O-Ren Ishii, in Quentin Tarantino's *Kill Bill: Vol. 1*. An American of Taiwanese descent, she emanates strength and vulnerability, just like the moon's energy this month. Protection, vulnerability, strength, and discretion are the words that come to mind when we think of the life of this artist, who is not only an actress, famous for her role in *Kill Bill* as well as her role in the television series *Ally McBeal*, but also a painter and visual artist known by her Chinese name, Yu Ling.

Her art, on exhibit in many international museums, includes painting, photography, and collage, a technique she has been dedicated to since childhood. Her wealth of resources is fascinating; she is a true *multipotentialite;* but at the same time, she is very reserved. It is as though the strength that she emits goes through her and takes shape beyond her and her personality and appears at the height of the project.

The same happens to the energy of the Moon of Winds, which is both warrior and child with a freshness that makes it attainable. This moon reminds us that we do not need to be aggressive in battle, that there is much strength and power to be found in a sprout that grows, in a work of art, or in a meadow in the spring. It reminds us of the gentle and reserved but deeply tenacious strength of those who take the road less traveled to carry their own unique message.

You can find inspiration in this moon if you find harmony between the aggressive and vulnerable energies, and in the determination that is inherent in every desire, that becomes reality not only with magic, but above all with effort, action, and direction. Lucy Liu has infused energy both in her art and in her choices, which have often been unconventional. In her and in the Moon of Winds I see the beauty of strength, sensitivity, and a passion that, instead of distorting, shines brighter and brighter, with perseverance and wholeness like a growing blade of grass.

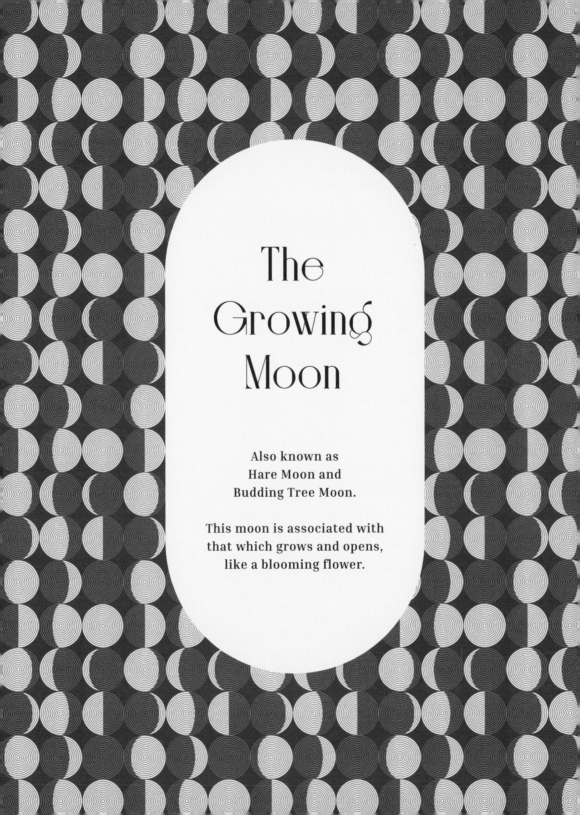

The Growing Moon

Also known as
Hare Moon and
Budding Tree Moon.

This moon is associated with
that which grows and opens,
like a blooming flower.

T he moon in April is the embodiment of spring. It represents a time of growth, nourishment, and fertility. The sun in April re-awakens completely and eases the harshness of winter. April makes you feel like walking barefoot on the first blades of newly sprouted grass, surrounded by new leaves, flowers, and nature itself.

The month of April brings a strong desire to dig your hands into the earth, to begin gardening again, to prepare the soil and to fertilize it, and to check on the seeds you planted in March. Your contact with nature is spontaneous. Just as the plants grow without tension in an act of necessity, we also feel the need to get out and connect to the trees, flowers, and animals, and to free our wild side.

Spring and the April moon are associated with virginity and, in fact, the triple goddess of neo-pagan symbolism represents three moments of life's phases: the virgin, the mother, and the crone. Spring is Botticelli's *Venus,* Aphrodite, as she is born from the foam of the sea. It reminds me of the Empress card of the *Wildwood Tarot* deck. The Empress is depicted as a priestess who transforms everything she touches, giving it new life. Her tongue is made of leaves that grow with whirlwind speed, like the leaves on the trees in this period.

The moon in April represents wild growth, like that in one of the corners of my garden. I prefer that my garden not be too orderly, so I promised myself (and the fairies that live nearby) that I would leave part of the terrain free, untidy, and uncultivated. Sweet wormwood, thistles, wild mint, clematis, dandelions, and yarrow grow there, and I find new plants every year. To leave room for growth is a balance between chaos and order, between observation and action. In this sense, the moon in April is the Growing Moon; it teaches you to participate in the process and enjoy it fully, whether it be in the forest or in your garden, or even on your terrace or windowsill!

Lunar Phases

WITH THE NEW MOON in April, prepare yourself to receive. Growth is a process that includes some pauses and takes place in relationship to the surrounding environment. Receiving, listening, and observing are as important as nourishing and growing. Dedicate the night of the New Moon to listening, meditating, and breathing. This is the time to focus on the roots of your dreams and to remember that they need nourishment to grow strong. Where will it come from?

DURING THE WAXING MOON in April, focus on the progress you have made and on the development of your projects. What point have you reached? What have you already accomplished and what remains for you to do? Buy some plant fertilizer to nourish your green friends, allow yourself a barefoot walk in a meadow, pick some flowers and bring them home, and leave gifts for the fairies in the gardens (or even in public flower beds!). This is the ideal moment to devote your attention to your garden, being careful to avoid comparing it to those of others, and to focus on your personal growth.

WITH THE FULL MOON in April, carry out your simplest projects, and if you have activities to finish, do them, and use the moon's energy to be productive and dynamic. If you can, go to a garden and make a circle with freshly picked wildflowers or with the flowers from your terrace. Place yourself at the center of the circle and, as you look at the moon, let its gentle strength regenerate you. Focus your attention on your body, a sacred temple, and celebrate it. Remember that who you are is the starting point for the development of all your projects.

DURING THE WANING MOON in April, reflect on what you need to grow and on what is blocking you. Use these days to take stock and make decisions that lighten your step and clear your way. Try to understand which obstacles you can turn into opportunities and which ones can only be hindrances or burdens to let go of.

Plant

Every part of the dandelion represents growth, from its taproot that explores the depths of the earth, to its brightly colored flower that reminds us of the April sun, and, above all, to the winged seeds that come from its strange fruit, called a *pappus*, that fly lightly on the wings of the wind and desire. Dandelions often grow in the cracks in concrete, and it is common to see them sprout between one step and another, or from the fissures in the road. Growth, perseverance, and optimism are the keywords associated with the plant.

Another characteristic of the plant is the polymorphism of its leaves, which means that not all dandelions have the same leaves. In fact, they come in a variety of shapes and sizes. The dandelion likes to experiment!

The dandelion plant has digestive and diuretic properties, a veritable cure-all for the spring season that helps regenerate the blood and drain the liver. It helps us free our bodies of toxins and to clear out the remains of winter. Add tender leaves to a salad, or use the flowers to decorate your spring dishes. You can pickle the flower buds to make tasty dandelion capers, and you can use the flowers and sugar to make a golden yellow syrup that is both delicious and depurative.

The dandelion is very adaptable. It continues to grow in fields that are mowed often because it regulates its height in order to stay below the blade of the mower. The message of the dandelion is contained in the concept of perseverance, which does not mean resisting at all costs, but rather understanding which small changes you can make, and knowing how to choose between what is difficult but possible and what is unhealthful for your soul.

Remember to smile at every dandelion flower you see, and it will smile back at you!

Dandelion

Taraxacum officinale

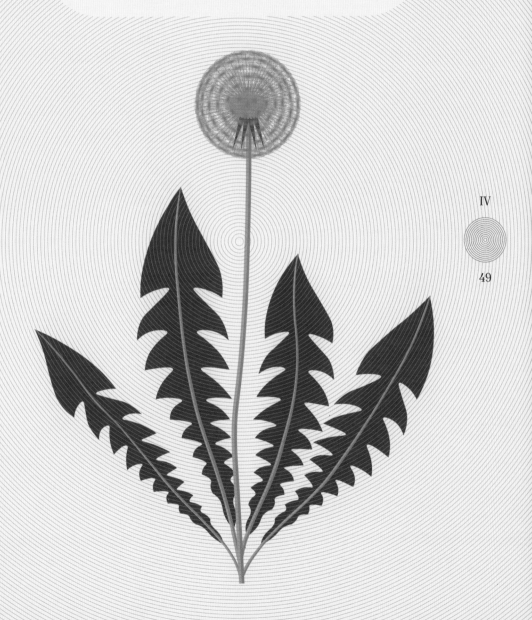

IV

49

Symbols

HARE

The hare is associated with the April moon because of its fertility and because of the speed at which it moves, just like the speed and sponta-neity with which leaves, plants, and buds grow in this season.

EGG

The egg is one of the quintessential symbols of spring. It represents the inception, birth, and shell that breaks open to give way to a new life. Easter eggs contain a surprise that reminds us of the spirit of the April moon, playful and unpredictable.

YELLOW AND PINK

The colors of this moon are yellow, like the first sun in April and like the dandelion's flower; but according to the doctrine of signatures, yellow is also associated with the liver and its purification, while pink is tender and sensual like Aphrodite.

THE EMPRESS

The Tarot card associated with this moon is without doubt the Empress. The card is number III in the deck, representing creation, chaos, and the sometimes uncontrolled vital strength, the loving push that is im-plicit in every flower that blooms and every sprout that grows in fertile soil.

FAIRIES

The Little People are associated with the month of April and its wild side. It is said that fairies inhabit uncultivated gardens, so we should leave a small piece of our garden (or a pot on our terrace) to grow freely and spontaneously for the fairies to live in.

Practices and Rituals

Prepare seed bombs by mixing one part green clay and one part soil with the seeds of flowers you love, and some water. Use the mixture to make little balls and, when they are dry, throw them into yards, parks, and flower beds to celebrate spring and its reawakening.

When you find a dandelion, look at it closely and ask yourself if it has developed in height or in width. What are its leaves like? What is the soil like where it is growing? Ask yourself what you can learn from its bearing and from your observations.

Buy a bouquet of flowers and take it home to celebrate spring.

Add some edible wild herbs to your diet (only the ones you know are not harmful); put some fresh flowers in your salad and some rosebuds in your tea.

To make a syrup with violets, pick the flowers and put them in a jar filled with cold water, and let them steep for two hours. Filter your infusion and heat it over a fire until it is reduced by about half. Then add one or two spoons of honey and an equal amount of brandy to help preserve the syrup. The syrup can be used for a cough, but also to gain a wider vision and to heal your heart.

Find a tree you like and hug it. If the branches are sturdy enough, you can also try to climb it.

Leave gifts for the Little People in the park, such as little bells, ribbons tied to the trees, honey, and dried fruit.

Remember that to grow, you must also observe, wait, and adapt. Keep a little diary where you note the progress of your projects. Every time you reach a goal, celebrate your success.

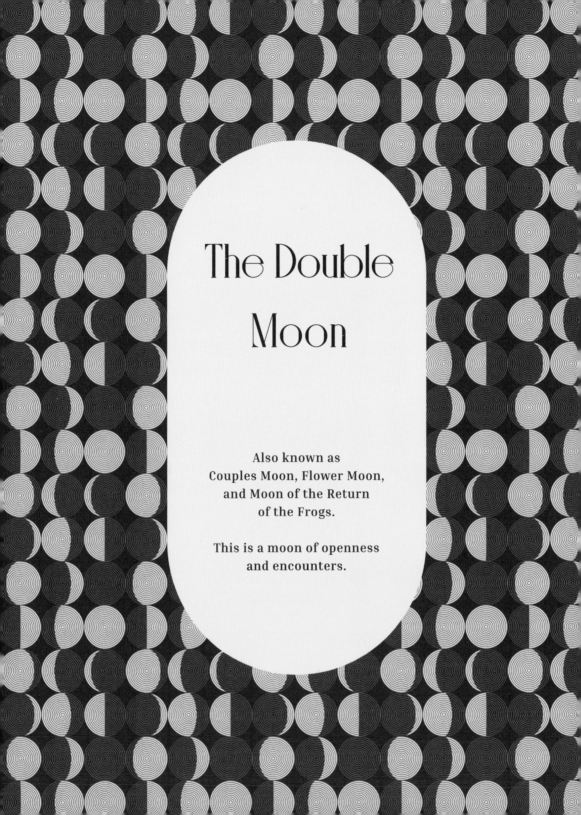

The Double Moon

Also known as
Couples Moon, Flower Moon,
and Moon of the Return
of the Frogs.

This is a moon of openness
and encounters.

In May, you might be showered with a rain of petals as you walk outdoors, or you might see a tree that was bare yesterday and has suddenly bloomed, or encounter a fragrance that takes you home, in your heart, which for me is the scent of the roses that grow next door.

May is a month of receptiveness when our bodies respond to the light, to the color of the flowers, to the softness of the petals, and to the great desire to open up. Breathe deeply, expand your chest, and make your heart a welcoming place where you can meet the heart of others.

Traditionally, May 1 was the day of Beltane, named for the Celtic god Belenos or Belenus, the god of light, fire, and the sun. Night fires were lit to honor him and to win love and fertility. This is a time for pleasure, to be aware of your senses and of exchanges. With this moon's energy, we are ready to meet and fall in love. May is the ideal month for exploring love, including self-love, a love that can save the world. Focus on your body, take care of pleasure, listen to it, and let yourself be guided by sensation and not by reason. Under the light of the May moon, we can fall in love, with ourselves or perhaps with another.

The Maypole represented the union between the Sun God and the Earth God. It was consecrated with a dance in which the participants held red and white ribbons that were tied to the pole, symbolizing the forces of life and death winding together to grant a new life. After the wild dancing, participants jumped over a fire to receive their blessing; and during the night, couples met in woods surrounded by bonfires to make love, calling to mind the sacred bond between the sky and the earth and celebrating it with pleasure.

lunar Phases

WITH THE NEW MOON in May, you can sever relationships that no longer nourish you or that have become toxic. Whether it be an ex, a co-worker, or a friend who turned out not to be, use the energy of this New Moon to cut ties with them and the attachment to them that you feel inside. Devote time and energy to the relationships that make you feel good; do it as part of your self-care and as an act of necessary love.

DURING THE WAXING MOON in May, dedicate yourself to the relationships that are germinating now and that you want to cultivate with small gestures and kindness and a smile. If there is someone that you like but that you do not know well, the time is right to invite that person to get a drink together or take a walk or simply to talk. This is the moment to give your love to those who make you feel good, to give preference to relationships that are still budding and watch them grow in the coming months.

V

57

WITH THE FULL MOON in May, celebrate the abundance of what you have and of the love around you. You are surrounded by people who love you, and it is never too late to show them that you also feel love, gratitude, and joy. Find time for those you care about, for your best friend, and for the one you love. Demonstrate your passion for the things you love, and feed the flame.

DURING THE WANING MOON in May, experience your inner warmth and find time to fall in love with yourself. Make yourself an excellent candlelit dinner and spend time alone to discover what you like to do, and do it. Give yourself over to love and pleasure.

Plant

R oses have been used in medicine and cosmetics since ancient times. Dioscorides was a doctor and botanist in ancient Greece. He indicated the rose as a remedy with cooling, astringent properties, characteristics that are still acknowledged today. In Ayurvedic medicine, the rose is used to calm with kindness and to nourish with sweetness, with effects that are both invigorating and soothing. The rose strengthens the heart; it grants kind courage and promotes mental and spiritual clarity.

The rose is associated with Venus and Mars—and, of course, with love, which it long has symbolized. Its thorns, sacred to the god Mars, defend the rose and teach us that no healthy love can exist if you do not protect your boundaries and individuality. To love means to fly close to one another while keeping your own route, without ever losing sight of your own personality, needs, and, above all, self-love. The flower of the rose plant is sacred to Venus and represents pure pleasure, softness, and voluptuousness. The rose is said to have aphrodisiac properties and is used in many recipes for elixirs, liqueurs, and love potions.

The rose is the guardian at the gates of our hearts and its energy is one of openness. It starts at the center just like its buds and opens up like a heart in love. Like all aphrodisiac plants, its powers are relaxing and nutritious, in perfect harmony with the influence of Venus. It is associated with the concept of beauty and is used in creams, face tonics, perfumes, and oils.

The rose carries a double message: "Love and defend." The rose, whose nature includes thorns as well as petals, asks you to love yourself totally, exactly as you are and in all your parts. It tells you to wear your thorns proudly and open your heart as much as you want.

Rose

Rosa gallica, damascena, Rosa x damascena

V

59

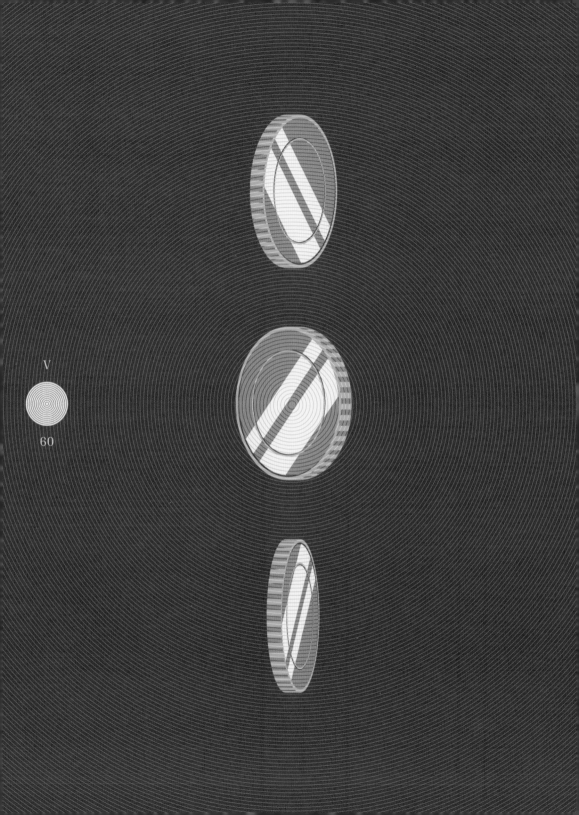

Symbols

RIBBONS

Colored ribbons, preferably made of satin, are associated with this moon, in part because of their use on the Maypole, and in part because they were used in the ritual of handfasting, a pagan wedding in which the spouses' hands are tied together with ribbons. Ideally, handfasting is celebrated in this season.

HAWTHORN

A magical tree that blooms in this period, the hawthorn is associated with the heart, both because of its beneficial effects on your heart's rhythm and on your blood pressure, and because of its link to the Little People, an enchanted realm that celebrates the return of the light in this season. Like the rose, hawthorns have thorns and beautiful flowers.

CROWNS OF FLOWERS

During the rituals of Beltane, crowns made of blossoms and ribbons were worn to celebrate the wholeness of nature, the flowers, the colors, and the joy that lights up this month.

THE LOVERS

The Tarot card associated with this moon is the Lovers: an encounter, a choice. The card has a dual nature, just like this moon, because when we meet another, there is always a choice to be made, as well as a comparison between who we are and who we want to become.

GOLD

The color associated with this moon is gold, the color of light, of the sun at the height of its splendor, of the fire that shines, and of abundance. Gold coins are also associated with this moon. They symbolize wealth and gratitude for everything that exists.

Practices and Rituals

Gather rose petals and scatter them on the doorstep of the person you love, as a coming-home surprise. Do the same on your own doorstep so only love can get in.

Braid a crown with flowers picked in a field and let them dry. You can burn it in fire when midsummer comes, to liberate its energy.

Go out dancing, or, if you do not like to dance at the club, make yourself a playlist you love and dance, unchained, in your favorite room of the house!

Invent a benediction for your creative tools. This moon protects and increases creativity, so this is the ideal time to bless your notebooks, brushes, or kitchen tools.

Use rose petals in your seasonal salads.

Find a hawthorn tree and spend some time with it; connect with the enchanted spirits.

Take care of your body, love it wholly, just as it is. Give yourself a beauty treatment—a massage with scented oils or a rose-petal scrub.

Hang a crystal prism in your window and fill your house with rainbows.

Make a list of the checkups you need, because prevention is one of the best ways to truly take care of ourselves.

Write a love letter to the person you will be five years from now. Then, write another one to the person you were five years ago. Put them in separate envelopes with some rose petals.

David Bowie

Track: "Starman" (from the album *The Rise and Fall of Ziggy Stardust and the Spiders from Mars*, 1972)

V

64

Pop Icon

When I was just a child, I met David Bowie on the street. He was in town for a concert, and I ran into him and his wife Iman (and their bodyguards). What I remember most, besides the excitement I felt knowing I would see him in concert that evening, was the light. He was twinkling, as though something magical was floating around him. It must have been light, I am sure of it.

Just like Belenus, David Bowie came from fire, from the lightning bolt that symbolized his creative power and was part of his memorable makeup.

Born Robert David Jones, he was an incredible, multifaceted artist who successfully re-created himself many times during his career. He played a number of instruments, painted, and acted, and was able to convey his passion in all the things he did and explored. His costumes were true works of art, including a famous one designed for him by Kansai Yamamoto, and he inspired a deck of Tarot cards, drawn and produced by Davide De Angelis.

In him, the light of the Double Moon shines. This moon can bring you inspiration along the path of your passion, and it reminds you that magic is a feat accomplished with your will and your openness to opportunity.

Just like the rose and the spirit of this moon, David Bowie is both flower and thorn, the demonstration that anything is possible, which is the subtitle to the movie *Labyrinth,* where he played the Goblin King.

This moon, more than any other, reminds us that shadow and light can coexist; that birth and death are not far from each other; that passion, just like the North Star, can always lead us home to our hearts.

The Honey Moon

Also known as
Pink Moon, Moon of the Sun,
and Strawberry Moon.

The moon in June is one of
expansion, and its energy
is that of midsummer
and of the solstice,
the longest day of the year.

When I think of June, I think of an enchanted painting called *Flaming June* by Frederic Leighton. In it, a girl dressed in flaming orange rests, curled up in an armchair. Despite the apparent calm, the strength of this month can be felt; and the moon is its expression, the beauty of simply being, of being present, and of openness and exploration.

After the spring with its quiver of vibrant life and its focus on growth, this month's moon and the arrival of summer allow us to finally rest, to observe, and to be aware of what we have and enjoy it fully. The time is right to go from the *what could be* of spring to the *being here and now* of summer.

During the month of June, medicinal herbs reach the height of their potency. For almost all herbs, the balsamic period—or the period in which their concentrations of active substances are at their highest— is summer, especially midsummer and the solstice, from June 21 to 24. Just like the herbs, we also use our time in summer to carry out projects and intentions that we imagined during the spring. We rediscover our connection to the daily magic of the light and the power of fire and love.

The moon in June connects us to the element of fire and to light itself. The days grow longer and we have time to experiment with what we have learned so far, to dare, and to take action. This is a period for exploration. We want to stay outdoors, lured by the fragrances, flowers, and butterflies that fly from blossom to blossom. It is a time for searching and for openness in the face of what is new and uncharted. This month, characterized by sun and warmth, suggests that we bring our true essence into the light together with our soul and our own unique expressiveness.

Even the nights are brighter, and we can take evening walks. With the mild climate, these walks become magical explorations, sometimes in the company of fireflies who, like the moon, remind us that magic is all around us.

Lunar Phases

WITH THE NEW MOON in June, work on being receptive to love. Ask yourself what you need to feel loved and what traits your ideal person might have. Then try to develop these inclinations in yourself. We attract that which vibrates in our own energy; your vibe attracts your tribe! During this New Moon, tune into what you desire and cultivate it, starting now.

DURING THE WAXING MOON in June, it is opportune to stock up on the energy and light you will need during the winter months. Your actions are direct and determined, and you can accomplish what you have planned until now. Increase your personal energy, for example, by waking up a half hour earlier in the morning to do yoga or to have an unhurried breakfast. You can wake up at dawn and watch the sun rising. Think of the plans you made in previous months and what you can do now to actualize them.

WITH THE FULL MOON in June, find your connection with fire. The message of this moon is life and presence, like a fire that burns, healing and transforming matter into energy. Reflect about where the sacred fire of your life lies. What is the passion that feeds you and what can you do to keep the flame alive forever? Light a small, protected fire in a large pot or other fireproof container to emulate the fires of Saint John, who celebrated the summer solstice.

DURING THE WANING MOON in June, think of what you can accomplish now to actualize your projects, without the fear of taking a few risks. This is the time to try something you have never done before, change your habits, take a different way to work, talk to strangers, watch a movie that attracts you but scares you, and so on. Be imaginative and daring.

Plant

The origin of the scientific name of St. John's wort, *Hypericum perforatum*, is disputed. Linnaeus attributed it to the Greek words *hyper* and *eikon*, which together mean "over the image" and relate to the shape of the petals of the plant and to the impression that there is an image on them. The word *perforatum* refers to the small resinous sacs on the leaves that look like small flowers against the light.

The feast day of Saint John the Baptist on June 24 is the best time to pick this particularly special plant. According to popular traditions, the plant provided protection against the devil and could cleanse negative energies from people and places. Its curative powers speak to us with the same language. In external use, it is useful for healing wounds and soothing burns; and taken internally, it is one of the most effective plant remedies for depression.

The plant is very potent and interacts with many medications, so it must be taken under the supervision of an herbalist, but it brings light to the darkness of depression, which is no more than the obscurity of our soul. St. John's wort releases the summer sun that it condenses in its petals to help us face the coldest months. It can be used to make a special oil, known as St. John's oil (oil of hypericum), an effective remedy for rashes, burns, and redness. Its warming, comforting effects bring us the sun of June during the winter months.

The message of St. John's wort is: "Remember that a small light shines within you, even when the night seems to be at its darkest."

St. John's Wort

Hypericum perforatum

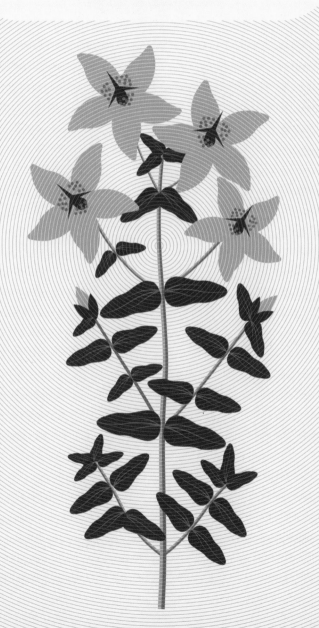

VI

72

Symbols

BEES AND BEEHIVES

The moon in June evokes honey and the work of the bees as they fly from flower to flower, bringing life with growth and encounters with others. Honey is rich and nutritious, just like the sun in June that provides us with a reserve of warmth for the winter months.

FEATHERS

Red or orange feathers symbolize prosperity, the element of air, communication, and growth, the fleetingness of touch, and the sense of lightness that characterizes this season of the year.

STRAWBERRIES

Strawberries are a symbol of newness and love and, according to a Cherokee legend, they are also linked to romance. They are associated with this moon because of their fresh and playful nature and their links to children, infancy, and innocence.

THE CHARIOT

The Tarot card associated with this moon is the Chariot, which symbolizes ambition and success, movement toward the light, change, and transformation. The card is magical and dynamic, just like this moon.

RED AND ORANGE

Red and orange are associated with this moon because of their connection to fire and sensuality. They are the colors of the first two chakras, which are the centers of foundation and sexual energy. Dynamic and energetic, they bring to mind fire and heat.

FIRE

Fire is the element associated with the moon in June because it is mobile, transformative, and bright. Fire is willpower, desire, passion, energy, and heat; it heals wounds and brings light.

Practices and Rituals

Eat a ray of sun, literally. Stand in the sunlight and imagine that you are eating the rays. Let them illuminate your face and your lips, and let the light fill you.

Practice generosity. This is the time when everything is luxuriant and, like the plants that give us the gift of their fruit, we can give to others—an afternoon off, a cup of coffee with a loved one, a book that we loved and want to share, or a delicious lunch.

Gather the herbs of the solstice—St. John's wort, meadow sage, sweet wormwood, verbena, and the many others you can find this season. Always be careful to respect the environment and its resources when you do.

Create sun decorations made of paper or light fabric to hang around the house. Hang them in the windows; place them on your personal altar or bedside table, wherever you want to bring the energy of the sun.

Buy a beautiful bouquet of sunflowers.

Wash your face with morning dew collected from the plants that grow near your house. At one time, this practice was considered a powerful spell that would grant eternal youth.

Take a moon bath; in your swimsuit, lie down under the moon's rays and soak them in. If you are near the seashore, take a moonlit swim and let the night waters lull you.

Wake up at dawn, light a candle, and enjoy the performance of the light as it grows.

Celebrate the love in your life; sentimental love, erotic love, the love of friends and community, and the love of the animals and plants that live on this planet with you.

VI

75

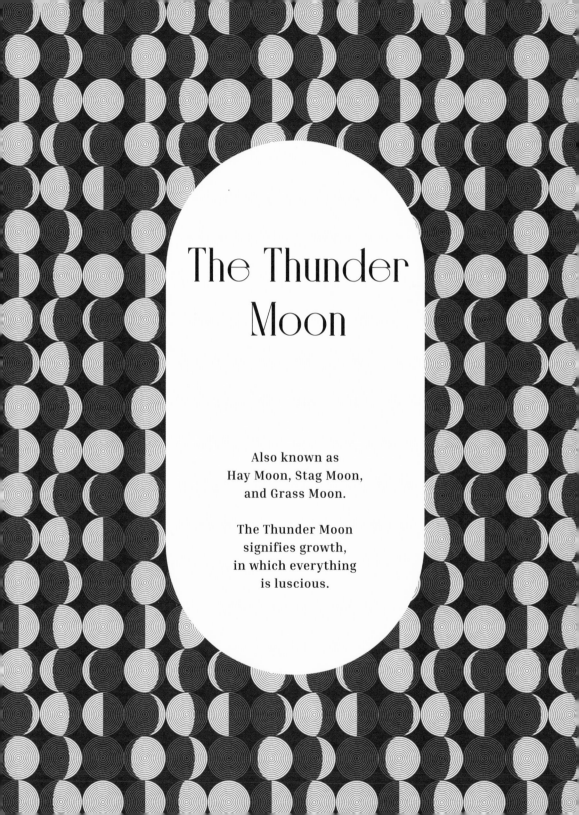

The Thunder Moon

Also known as
Hay Moon, Stag Moon,
and Grass Moon.

The Thunder Moon
signifies growth,
in which everything
is luscious.

T he moon in July is named for Thunder, for obvious reasons. This is the month of frequent summer storms like the kind that make you think you might be in Kansas, ready for a trip to the magical Kingdom of Oz, in the middle of a tornado. In July, the skies often fill with rain and the clouds turn as black as night, but then, in an instant, the sun is shining again on the wheat in the fields and on the herbs ready to be picked.

July makes us think of water, a vital element whose origins we often lose track of even though it is where we, as human beings, come from. A mother's womb holds the waters of life, just as the earth with its streams and springs brings us one of the fundamental elements we need to survive.

Do you ever stop to wonder where the water that comes from your faucet originates? That before flowing into an aqueduct somewhere in the mountains, it was gushing from a spring? A summer storm is an opportunity to connect with water in the most instinctual way. It is electric, sudden, and sensorial. It reactivates our energy; it calls us outdoors to feel the drops of rain as they wet our skin, and reconnect with our inner selves.

The Thunder Moon encourages us to keep in touch with our instincts and to let our wild side foster us. The water that this moon brings is the juice of the plants, of the cells that make the flower petals swell, the thirst-quenching water that favors growth and prosperity. It is the juice of a mango eaten in the sun's rays, and it is the same water that readies the plants for harvest, full of essential oils and healing powers. It is a whole, complete water that grows just like the moon that moves it.

The moon in July comes when the deer's antlers are at the height of their growth, reminding us that we should not be afraid to grow or express our true nature. "Be as you are," it whispers, "and have no fear."

Lunar Phases

WITH THE NEW MOON in July, the energy is right to ask yourself who you really are and how you want to come into the world. How can you bring out your true nature, whether it be from a personal point of view or in relationships or in your community? This is the time to reveal the most hidden parts of your heart, to find the courage to decide how you want to live in your surroundings. Pick a card from a deck of divination cards and ask it to reveal that which you want to see but that is not yet visible.

DURING THE WAXING MOON in July, water all of your plans with the water of emotions. Devote yourself to the things you have to do on a daily basis, and do them in whatever way makes you feel better. Spend time planning actions that bring you well-being now and put them into practice. The power of the Thunder Moon electrifies and excites you. Identify what inspires you and dedicate time to your care and well-being.

WITH THE FULL MOON in July, celebrate your first harvest of the year. What have you obtained with your efforts? What completely ripened fruits do you get to taste? It is very important to stop everything for a moment and honor your successes, to take a look at what you have achieved and celebrate it. During this Full Moon, you can.

DURING THE WANING MOON in July, prepare to receive ideas for new projects. Just like a summer storm that rages and cools and then leaves a rainbow in its path, try to imagine what is on the path of your future, without limiting yourself. Dare to dream with your eyes open. Be receptive to subtle messages and heed coincidences and concurrences. Listen to the rain and learn its song.

Plant

The elderberry tree is considered sacred, wise, and magical in many cultures. It has a strong connection to lightning and is sometimes planted near the home as a protection against it. In Russia, people traditionally hang bundles of flowers, leaves, and berries of the tree on their doors for good luck.

The elderberry has strong ties to the enchanted world of sprites, elves, and all the creatures of the Little People. Spend the night of the summer solstice under an elderberry tree, and you might meet the king and queen of fairies with their band of nymphs, gnomes, and leprechauns.

According to Celtic pagan traditions, the elderberry tree represents the three faces of the goddess: in the spring, the virgin with her multitude of flowers; in the summer, the mother and her luscious purple berries; and in the autumn, the old crone who has lost her leaves. It alludes to the cyclic nature of the rhythm of life and its changes.

The elderberry tree expresses dual properties; its flowers are associated with Venus and express beauty, harmony, and regulation. They are used to lower a fever and balance body temperature, as well as to flavor sweets, beverages, and breads. The purple berries are associated with Saturn and are slightly toxic. They can only be ingested when they are completely ripe, and only when cooked. The berries make a wonderful, dark-purple-colored jam. The other parts of the plant are toxic or poisonous.

The elderberry tree makes us think of life as a circle that moves in spirals of growth and transformation. It suggests that everything that happens, happens for our evolution, and that we can dance with life in harmony with its cycles.

The elderberry's message is: "Treasure the past, dream of the future, and stay in the present."

Elderberry

Sambucus nigra

VII

81

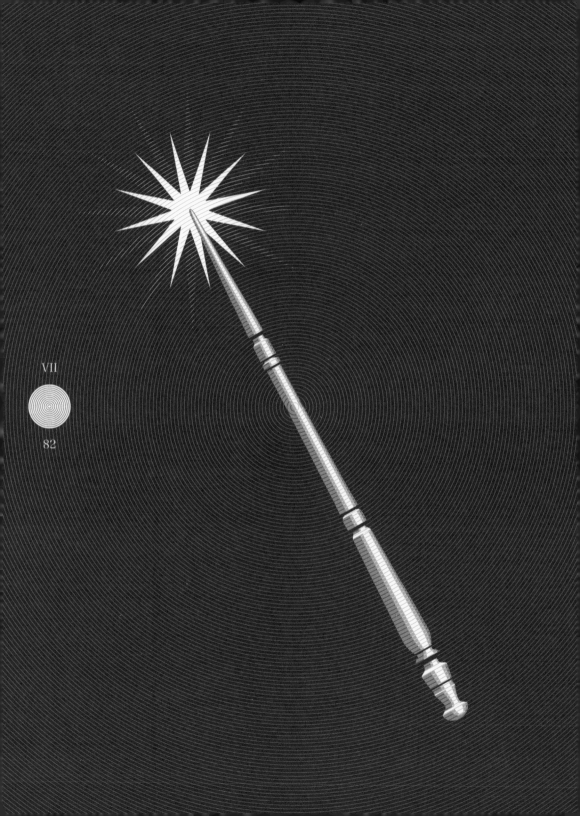

VII

82

Symbols

BODIES OF WATER

Water is of the utmost importance to this moon, and bodies of water are its primary symbol. Not only lakes, streams, and oceans, but even the small puddles of water left by summer storms. All of them are doors to the world of the imaginary. Look at your reflection in them and think about how it feels to see life backward.

DRIED HERBS

Bundles of lavender, St. John's wort, mint, melissa, and other medicinal herbs characterize this season, when their harvest is favorable. The concentration of active ingredients in the plants is at its peak, just like the vital energy of this season.

CIRCLE

In July, the first harvest takes place—the wheat harvest. The harvest brings to mind the cyclic nature of life, which is not a straight line but a pathway of evolution through release and rebirth, the symbol of which is the circle.

MAGIC WAND

This is the best instrument for making wishes come true and for directing our actions and energies in the direction we wish to take.

THE TOWER

The Tarot card associated with this moon is the Tower. The card represents the destructive and regenerative force of the storm, the immediacy of lightning and of clear vision. It reminds us that it is impossible to always have everything under our control.

LIGHT GREEN OR PURPLE

The colors of this moon are the light green of summer leaves and the purple of elderberries, colors that combine communication and intuition.

Practices and Rituals

When the first summer storm comes, go out and get wet in it. Stop for a few moments and savor the feeling of every drop on your skin. Be aware of the beauty of your body in its connection to nature.

Find a fallen tree branch and use it to make a magic wand. Use string, stones, small shells, little bells, and anything else your imagination suggests.

Take a walk around an open market and buy some local, organic, seasonal food.

Construct a kite and let it fly high in the July wind.

Write a gratitude list with all the things you are thankful for and take time to celebrate the goals you have achieved.

Pursue causes you believe are just; become active in your neighborhood and do not be afraid to promote your opinions.

Offer small gifts to the fruit trees and plants you find along your way, nourishing them with fertilizer and quenching their thirst with water if they need it.

Make a rain stick with a piece of bamboo. Put a handful of rice, some seashells, and some nutshells inside the bamboo and close the open end with foil or tape, then tip the stick from end to end and listen to the sound of the rain. You can cover your stick with colored fabric, ribbons, or decorated paper.

Make a mandala with seeds and wheat spikes and let the summer storm scatter it.

Remember that you are made of stars and lightning bolts. Honor the magic of intuition and of the unexpected.

Nina Simone

Track: "I Put a Spell on You"
(from the album *I Put a Spell on You*, 1965)

Pop Icon

The Thunder Moon is a moon of celebration and power. Its unexpected, electrifying energy brings out the talent in each of us. It is not afraid to show itself for what it is and to take uncomfortable positions.

We can find the same quality in life and in the vibrant voice of Nina Simone, in her deep notes that are as intense as a storm, in the emotions she conveys, and in her vibrations.

Nina Simone is a singer, pianist, writer, and activist for civil rights in the United States. Her musical career and her activism make her the embodiment of the characteristics of this particular moon.

Just like the moon, she has always known when to show herself and when to disappear, without ever losing her personal battle. She is an active feminist and was a friend of Martin Luther King Jr. and Malcolm X. Her singing has been both a form of art and a form of political and civic activism.

Like a storm, like thunder, it is impossible to listen to Nina Simone's voice and not feel moved in some way.

Let yourself be moved by her and by the Thunder Moon; live intensely and put your ideas into action with clarity and strength. Dive into the notes of one of her songs and focus on the causes you believe to be just. Then try to imagine one small act to perform and do it, because with small steps you can change the world.

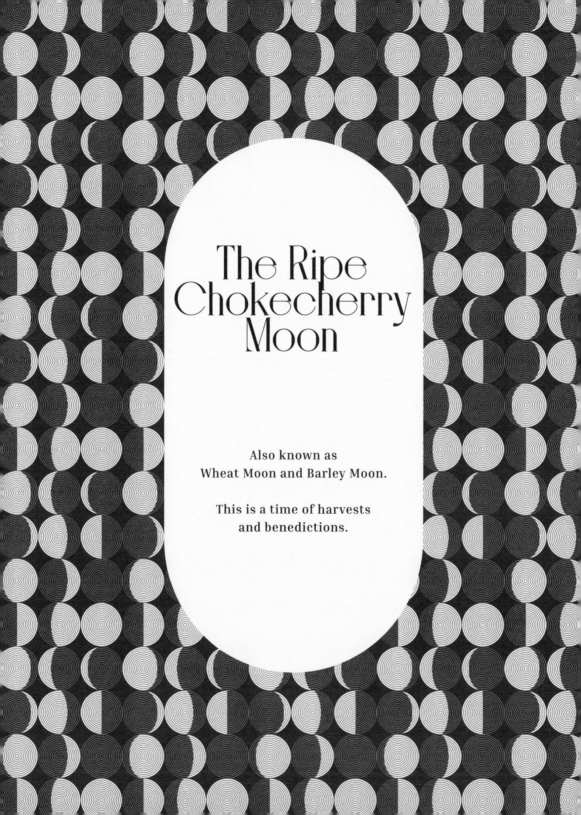

The Ripe Chokecherry Moon

Also known as
Wheat Moon and Barley Moon.

This is a time of harvests
and benedictions.

In August, the harvest is in full swing. As the wheat turns golden and fruit gets ripe, sugary, and nutritious, the chokecherries that give this moon its poetic name turn red. This moon represents the harvest, gratitude, and awareness of the abundance that surrounds us.

The moon in August represents the fullness of summer and gives us a glimpse of the autumn that is about to arrive. It invites us to enjoy every moment and to put something away for the cold months ahead. August, the month in which we celebrate the grain harvest, is the ideal month for harvesting what we have planted, both in the earth and in our daily lives. As some of its names suggest, there is a strong bond between this moon and grains, such as wheat and barley. They are the symbols of nourishment and rebirth—the wheat spike dies, but it also gives new life with its seeds.

The pagan Feast of Lughnasadh is celebrated in August to honor Lugh, the sun god incarnated in grain as a symbol of death and rebirth.

The wheat harvest is tied to the phases of the moon. Hildegard of Bingen was a nun and herbalist who lived in the 1100s. She wrote: "The grain cut during the waxing moon provides more flour than that harvested during the waning moon, because the waxing moon possesses all of its power, while the power of the waning moon is somewhat diminished. On the contrary, if the wheat has to maintain its germination potential, it is better to harvest it during the waning moon."

Baking bread brings us closer to this moon, making the dough and giving it time to rise, then tasting it as we savor its rich fragrance and being grateful for all we have and know how to do.

Have you ever picked fruit from a tree? Eating freshly picked fruit nourishes you, not only with its minerals and oligoelements, but also with the moon rays that lulled it at night, the sun that warmed it, and the flight of the butterflies that brushed against it.

There is much to be grateful for and to celebrate when we can connect with nature and the rhythms of slow living. The August moon is generous and shines brightly; it teaches you to take what you deserve and be grateful for what you have.

Lunar Phases

WITH THE NEW MOON in August, find a space in which to observe the abundance that surrounds you. The New Moon is always a good time to let go. Use the energy of this moon to abandon feelings of inadequacy and limitations about your success and earning capabilities. Be grateful for what you have. Make a list of all the small gifts you have received in past days: a piece of fruit, fallen from the tree; a cup of coffee offered to you at the café; or the flight of a butterfly. Reflect on the lavishness of the gift and on your ability to receive.

DURING THE WAXING MOON in August, you can imbue your projects with energy; the moment is ideal for giving a boost to what we want. Use this vibrant energy to concentrate on the experiences you are living and make them dynamic; and at the same time, ask yourself what really nurtures you. Make an outline that focuses on everything you need to develop what you are doing now, and identify where to direct your energies. Remember to wait for the right moment; just like the bread dough that must have time to rise, patience is part of success.

WITH THE FULL MOON in August, celebrate your wealth and your true nature. What are your resources? What are your strong points? How can you show them to the world? To celebrate this moon, make some magic bread dough and infuse it with your positive intentions as you knead. Watch it rise, and experience the pleasure of eating it straight out of the oven.

DURING THE WANING MOON in August, think about what you want to preserve for the cold months ahead. What part of this moment do you want to keep? What do you want to enjoy now, and what would you rather enjoy later? Make magic preserves with the fruit you pick in August; flavor it with your dreams and your wishes for the coming months. Remember to rest.

Plant

I have chosen to associate the pot marigold with the month of August because it is a veritable moon fire. Its orange color and some of its properties are obvious connections to the sun, but it also has connections to the moon. Its seeds are shaped like small crescent moons, and some of its properties are female and subject to lunar influence, making it like a gentle, intimate, homey fire.

The pot marigold has a particular resinous scent that is easily recognizable, and it leaves sticky, fragrant traces on your hand. One of my favorite summer rituals is to pick them and drink in their special perfume.

The pot marigold is also a generous, abounding plant. Its scientific name, *Calendula officinalis*, comes from the Latin word *calendae*, meaning the first day of the month. The Romans connected the word to the pot marigold because it commonly bloomed on the first day of every month throughout the summer if climate conditions were right. The flower of the pot marigold opens with the sun and closes in the shade, tracking the passage between light and obscurity. The plant grows very quickly, so it is easily associated with the August moon, the moon of growth and harvest.

The pot marigold is an ideal remedy for abrasions and redness of the skin. Used externally, it softens, soothes, and cures inflammations, but its internal use best expresses its lunar connections; it regulates the menstrual cycle and has beneficial effects on the female genital apparatus.

It helps bring things into balance and give them their appropriate importance. It can effectively treat frostbite and rashes, delicately restoring the body's warmth. The fact that it is hygroscopic makes it a weather predictor of sorts; it absorbs the humidity in the air and closes up if a storm is arriving. Its skin-healing properties make it useful in the treatment of slight injuries, burns, wounds, and rashes. It brings light and clarity.

Its message is: "Keep the fire lit in your nest and be grateful for all you have."

Pot Marigold

Calendula officinalis

VIII

94

Symbols

SUNFLOWER

The quintessential symbol of the sun, the sunflower resonates in this moon; its abundant production of seeds makes it an emblem of harvest, abundance, and gratitude.

GRAINS AND WHEAT SPIKES

The clearest symbol of this August Harvest Moon is cereal grains. They carry a message of nutrition, as well as one of death and rebirth; when the wheat is cut, its seeds give new life. At the same time, cereal grain crops are tied to a number of natural elements; if weather conditions are not favorable, there will be no harvest and thus no abundance. They are the symbol of care and foresight.

BREAD

This fundamental food has an intrinsic sacredness. It comes from the grain of the wheat, and we infuse our own personal energy into the dough as we prepare it. As it rises, it teaches us to rest. It is a treat for our palate and reminds us to savor the results of our efforts fully.

THE SUN

The Tarot card associated with this moon, the Sun, represents revelation, success, and gratitude. Its interpretation regarding light is an interesting one. What does it reveal about you? What do you want to bring out of the shadows?

ROSEMARY

This fragrant, resinous plant is hot and dry like the month of August. It has energizing, purifying properties, and it can be burned like incense to ward off negative energies.

Practices and Rituals

Make dinner for someone you love and try your hand at baking bread, even if you have never tried it before. Knead it for as long as you can: bread, sweets, dreams.

Make a moon tisane. Put a few pot marigolds in a cup of cold water and set it in the moon's rays overnight. The next morning, filter your tisane and drink it. Tune in to the sensations it transmits; full of lunar energies.

Invent a ritual to thank the plants that live with you or near you. Stay connected to your territory and observe the riches that surround you.

Make an oil with fresh pot marigolds. Put a handful of flowers in a container and cover them with sunflower oil. Leave it in the sun for three weeks and then filter it. Use the oil in the autumn to rediscover the intimate summer warmth of this month.

Let die that which has to die. If you let go of it, perhaps it will be transformed.

Celebrate fire, life, and wholeness in every shape.

Make a mandala of seeds and let the birds eat it.

Pick a sunflower and look at its seeds and the perfect spiral they form.

Make a night bonfire in a safe place and invite your friends to celebrate around it with you.

Collect seashells, sand, and stones at the seashore and put them in a glass jar. When winter comes, they will take you back to the seaside.

Be grateful. You are rich and you are brilliant.

VIII

97

The Changing Moon

Also known as
Wine Moon, Wheat Moon,
and Singing Moon.

This is a moon
of change and restitution.
The year changes pace here
and a connection to mysterious
inner energy is born.

In September, we can feel two forces that balance each other. The sun is still warm, but at night the air becomes crisp and the leaves begin to change and show off their red, orange, yellow, and gold pigments. The trees speak to the sunsets, and our personal motions become more heartfelt.

We can also perceive two forces in the plants: one flows toward the roots where nutrients and resources are accumulating for the winter months, and one flows toward the seeds that will reach maturity this month.

This is a moon of balance. When the autumn equinox arrives, generally on September 21, the day and the night are equally long; then, the hours of light begin to diminish. It is a moment of pause before we descend into the depths of ourselves and into mystery.

In the world of nature, this is the period when the seed is shaped and completed, making use of its summer experience. In much the same way, this moon encourages us to take stock, to organize the experiences the year has brought us so far, and to prepare for the colder, more introspective season to come.

The equinox represents balance and the assessment of energies, just as Virgo, the sign associated with this month, suggests. It is the moment in which our vision clears; we can see what we have accomplished up to now, where to direct our actions, and how to develop in the coming months. Equilibrium is more than assessment and balance: above all, it is finding harmony in situations that make us feel unbalanced. Ask yourself, "Okay, this is what I have now. I do not like it. What can I do to change it?"

The Changing Moon can help you define your point of balance, integrating aspects of light and shadow in the suspended moment that is September.

Lunar Phases

WITH THE NEW MOON in September, take inspiration from the trees and their falling leaves, a symbol of that which is no longer necessary. What relationships, projects, thoughts, or habits have become burdensome instead of stimulating and vitalizing? Take stock, and let go of what has become old and is no longer part of you.

DURING THE WAXING MOON in September, reflect about what you need to balance with growth and effort. What do you need to grow, to become equilibrated again? What are you overlooking? Think about your personal power and your strengths, and reflect on how you can mediate between them and your weaknesses. Equilibrate your forces, reduce your efforts, and let the energy flow. Observe your past to understand where you came from, to become aware of the progress you have made, and to stimulate your future moves from here on.

WITH THE FULL MOON in September, celebrate what you have harvested until now. This moon occurs during the month of the second harvest and of the seed; use its energy to honor the wealth that surrounds you and the provisions you have put away for the winter months. You will be happy to have them because, just like the preserves and jams you keep in the pantry, they will give you a taste of summer during the months of winter.

DURING THE WANING MOON in September, think about what you need to be equilibrated in terms of letting go and reducing your efforts. Where are you investing too much energy? What can help you re-equilibrate? Sometimes, putting excess effort into reaching a goal can be a warning light that indicates we are going in the wrong direction. This is a good time to evaluate our efforts and change direction if we have to.

Plant

Ivy is the plant that is most in harmony with this moon. It has a dual nature: it is lunar, growing as it does in the shade; but it's also solar, as it is always searching for the sun. It is customarily associated with Dionysus, like the grapes that are harvested in September to make wine, the nectar loved by this god of chaos, dance, life, and mystery.

The dual and balanced nature of ivy expresses the energies of the September moon. First, the plant develops sterile shoots with lobe-shaped leaves, and later, it produces fertile shoots with oval or lanceolate leaves. In autumn, when most plants go dormant, ivy has flowers that make it possible for bees to produce autumn honey.

Ivy is the quintessential symbol of adaptability and creativity. Its strength lies in its capacity to indulge, surpass, and transform every obstacle in its way, just like the walls of ruins that come alive and suggestive when ivy covers them with its leaves. Ivy's properties are also dual in nature. Only the birds like its poisonous berries, but its leaves have external uses in phytotherapy. They have significant draining and toning properties and, as a macerated oil, they are effective in treating cellulite blemishes and draining the lower limbs.

Ivy inspires our curiosity; it connects us to our ability to be free, to transform obstacles into opportunities, and to change. It helps us get over our fears and insecurities and become more flexible and more introspective.

The message of ivy is: "Shadow and Light are two faces of the same coin."

Ivy

Hedera helix

IX

103

IX

104

Symbols

WINE

Wine, the juice of grapes and the beverage of gods, hallowed by Dionysus/Bacchus, brings truth, intoxication, and the creative chaos of the Dionysian experience. It is used to celebrate and share, and it teaches us that equilibrium comes from measure.

DIONYSUS

The god associated with this period is Dionysus; a transformative divinity associated with wine, in part because of its developmental process, from fruit, to must, and ultimately to wine. It is also an expression of art and charisma, and I am (almost) sure that many rock stars, including Jim Morrison, have been the reincarnation of Dionysus.

DARK PURPLE

The color of this moon conveys mystery, profundity, and sacredness in a time when we are most in touch with ourselves and in which our personal inner quest is at its peak, after the extroversion of summer. Purple is the color of intuition, magic, and subtle thought.

YIN AND YANG

An ancient concept of balance between opposites, yin and yang teaches us that in the light, there is darkness and vice versa. Only with both parts can we find true balance, which is always dynamic.

APPLE

The apple is one of the symbols of the autumn equinox and is harvested this month, along with the last ripe plums.

TEMPERANCE

The Tarot card associated with this moon is Temperance, the card of equilibrium and alchemy. It suggests that to accomplish anything, opposites must be combined, mixed, and transformed. It is the only way to true harmony.

Practices and Rituals

Do autumn cleaning. Although it is less famous than spring cleaning, autumn cleaning is a useful practice. Donate warm clothes that you no longer use to someone who needs them. Prepare your living spaces for the winter months, taking notice of what needs to be fixed or replaced. Eliminate what is no longer useful.

Thank a tree that lives near you. Tie some ribbons to its branches, light some incense, offer it some fertilizer, or put some food for stray animals nearby. Hug the tree and feel the vital sap that is flowing to its roots.

Observe and balance your nights with your days. If you sleep too little or you wake up too late in the morning, or if your days are too hectic, remember to restore a healthy equilibrium between day and night.

Find out exactly when the equinox falls (around September 21) and invent a little practice to celebrate it.

Take productive pauses to perform small acts of care for yourself: read an article, make a beauty mask for your face, send a message to a loved one, or . . .

Organize your pantry with small reserves. Try to make some jam with the fruits of autumn, like plums, figs, and quinces. Adding flower petals will make it look like magic.

Pick some rosehips and string them onto a red thread to make a wild necklace.

Dedicate a night to unbridled dancing and let the Dionysian spirit whisk you away. Dance, jump, live, and let the chaos inspire you.

Remember that everything flourishes when its time comes, just like ivy. Find your moment and never worry about being late. You are not.

IX

107

Patti Smith

Track: "Dancing Barefoot" (from the album *Wave*, 1979)

Pop Icon

You can take inspiration from Patti Smith for this moon as it begins to trace its way toward the solemnity of the autumn months. A priestess of rock, Patti is a singer/songwriter, poet, and artist with something of the Dionysian about her. She mixes her music and poetry during her performances, exploring a connection to what is sacred.

Patti began her career when she was twenty-eight. In her book *Just Kids*, she reveals that her desire and her need to get up on stage and recite her poetry were inspired in part by a small Jim Morrison concert in the late '60s in New York.

Like the September moon that is a hub of energy, Patti Smith embodies the idea of change. At the height of her success as a rock 'n' roll artist, she began to experiment with new wave and punk—new resonant languages that would permeate her music. Patti's character has been volatile. When she began her artistic career, she did not want to be a singer. "I want to be a poet, not a singer," she told Robert Mapplethorpe, who answered, "You can be both."

Sometimes we can also be both; we can find a balance that allows us to fall outside an absolute definition and leaves us the freedom to be *this* and *that* together.

September's moon is magical and profound like Patti's voice, and it reminds us that staying connected to our dreams and our visions can be an inspiration for the whole world. Find space for your spirituality and remember to take a break from the frenzy of daily life and go to your sacred space. Try to write, like Patti, and let your writing bring out the messages of your soul. Cultivate what is sacred.

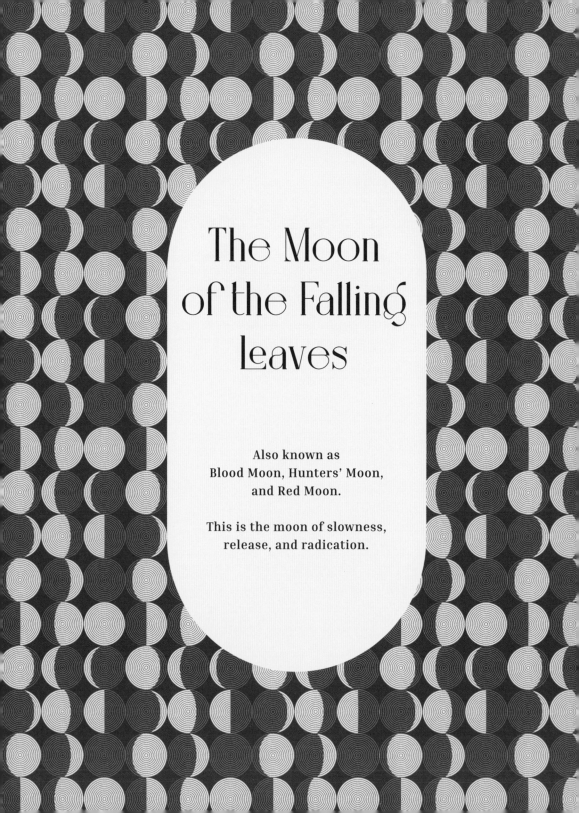

The Moon of the Falling Leaves

Also known as
Blood Moon, Hunters' Moon,
and Red Moon.

This is the moon of slowness,
release, and radication.

The month of October is important to the natural rhythm of the year, as the leaves fall from the trees and begin their transformation to fertile compost for new life. They accept their fall and their inactivity; and, like the leaves in October, we too must slow down and retire into our depths.

The October moon emanates a slow energy that pushes toward the earth, just like the myth of Persephone, daughter of Demeter, who was forced to live six months a year underground as a companion of Hades, the underworld god. We can ask ourselves what roots us. What mysterious message is the underworld whispering to us?

This moon is associated with the unknown; it falls in the same month as Halloween, also called Samhain, the time of the year when the veil between this world and the afterlife grows sheer and makes it easier to connect with what is not visible.

The moon in October has a strong connection to death and rebirth. The Celtic year ended on October 31 with the festival of Samhain, and the true beginning of the new year was with the New Moon in October.

This moon, which is closely affiliated with Libra and the scales, calls on us to weigh what we will keep and what we will let go in order to complete the transformation we have to make in the following month.

This moon makes us more receptive to invisible messages and more attentive to what our eyes cannot see. In many places in the world, October is the month when people celebrate their ancestors and those who no longer live among us. This is because it is the month when communications between the visible and the invisible become easier, and because we are at the end of a cycle, when reflecting about those who have gone becomes fundamental.

Our roots are found under the surface; and, just like the roots of plants, our hidden inner life becomes more active during this moon. During the months of autumn, plants store the elements they need for the winter; their lives move underground, where they will find the strength and energy to sprout again in the spring.

Lunar Phases

WITH THE NEW MOON in October, celebrate the birth of a new year and let go of what is no longer living. This New Moon is the perfect time to finish what belongs to the cycles that are coming to an end. Let go, accept the fall, and welcome the end. It is the only way to make way for the new; remember that digging up a root makes the plant die, but it also creates space for new life. Think about everything you need to let die, symbolically, in your life, and try to imagine what could take its place.

DURING THE WAXING MOON in October, learn to intercept the universe's subtle signals—passages in a book you are reading, songs you come across by chance, and manifestations of synchronicity. This is an ideal time to bring the messages of your dreams into real life and to trust your instincts. Remember, you need to listen with an open mind, without looking for instructions but rather simply receiving them spontaneously.

WITH THE FULL MOON in October, practice reconciliation and reconnection with those you have lost sight of or fallen out with. This powerful time of the year is ideal for rapprochement and softening your stance; be like the leaves that fall without resistance. Think about your sharp edges. What can you do to file them down? What stands in the way of reconciling with someone, and how can you take the first steps in that direction?

DURING THE WANING MOON in October, grant yourself some moments of solitude and personal re-energizing, take breaks, contemplate, and daydream. Learn to slow down and let go. We are in the habit of filling every minute of our days, including our free time; with this moon, experiment with *doing nothing* and see what happens.

Plant

T he pomegranate with its peculiar fruit is the plant that best represents the energy of this moon. Its spherical shape and great quantity of seeds make it a symbol of fertility and abundance. Its red juice, rich in vitamin C, is an allusion to blood and the vitality, strength, and energy still present in the autumn months.

The pomegranate is a symbol of both life and death. The Vietnamese say that when a pomegranate falls from the tree and breaks open, a hundred children will be born; but this ancient fruit is also the symbol of death, rebirth, and regeneration. In ancient cultures, it was offered to the dead as a promise of rebirth, and it can be seen on tombs throughout Greece and southern Italy. The dual nature of its symbology is reflected in the moon and its phases. Consider the myth of Persephone, the goddess who became the symbol of the changing seasons. The joy of her mother, Demeter, when Persephone was allowed to return from the underworld in spring, caused all things to begin growing again; and her despair, when Persephone had to go back in the winter, caused the plants and trees to fall into a deep, still sleep. This alternation of light and shadow resonates in the moon, between its full and new phases.

Ancient goddesses like Demeter or Aphrodite were often depicted holding the sacred pomegranate to symbolize their ability to bring life and death.

The pomegranate, particularly its juice, is a strong antioxidant that is effective in combating oxidative cell stress and, with it, aging. In addition to its beneficial effects for your heart, it eases stress, diabetes, and cardiovascular problems.

The message from the pomegranate is: "Honor every end; accept the void in order to allow for a new beginning."

X

114

Pomegranate

Punica granatum

X

115

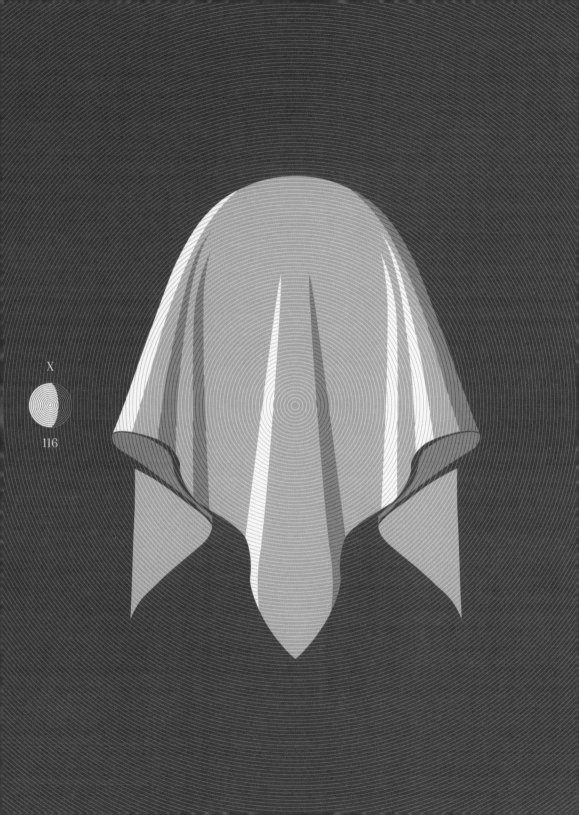

Symbols

LANTERNS

Lanterns light the way for the souls of the defunct in the nights of late October. They are magic and guidance in this very special month.

VEIL

The veil that separates this world from the next grows very thin at this time of year. Intuitive perceptions become clearer and you may meet with numerous synchronic events. This is a time of dreams and the imaginary.

JUSTICE

The Tarot card associated with this moon is Justice. At this time of year, we experience change, in which we must become aware of our own truth and of what we want to keep with us. Use the sword of Justice to cut away what is no longer necessary.

LIBRA

Libra is the zodiac sign associated with this period. Libra's ability to choose and to be truthful and its mediating force resonate in this time of the year; it transcends between worlds and listens to many languages.

MASKS

We dress up in scary costumes on the night of Halloween to acknowledge with fear; a cathartic practice that reveals what we are afraid of and how to manage our fear.

JACK O'LANTERN

The Anglo-Saxon tradition of carving a face on a pumpkin and putting a candle inside to illuminate its eyes, nose, and mouth is widespread in Europe. The practice originated with an Irish legend about a man named Jack.

Practices and Rituals

Use your creativity to carve a pumpkin for Halloween and then put a candle inside to celebrate these magical nights.

Make dinner for a silent guest; put an extra seat at the table in honor of those who are no longer in this world. Take a moment to think about your ancestors and let this little ritual be a secret message between you and them.

Turn off all the lights in your house one evening and go from room to room with a candle to bring light into the dark.

Try hard to give up a small habit that you want to get rid of.

Keep your phone off for half an hour during your day. Enjoy the quiet and take a break from being continuously connected.

This is a good month for divination. Get a deck of Tarot cards and pick one card from it every day. Take inspiration from the images you see, even if you do not know what they mean.

Make cookies for the night of the dead.

One evening, turn off all the lights and have a candlelit dinner. How does it change your perception of what you are eating? Pay attention to your senses.

Make your own runes. Runes were used by the Celts as a method of divination; they have beautiful symbols that are easy to reproduce. Draw your runes on small stones or engrave them on small wooden disks with a pyrography pen.

Cultivate your sixth sense in whatever way you like.

Celebrate your life and all there is left.

X

119

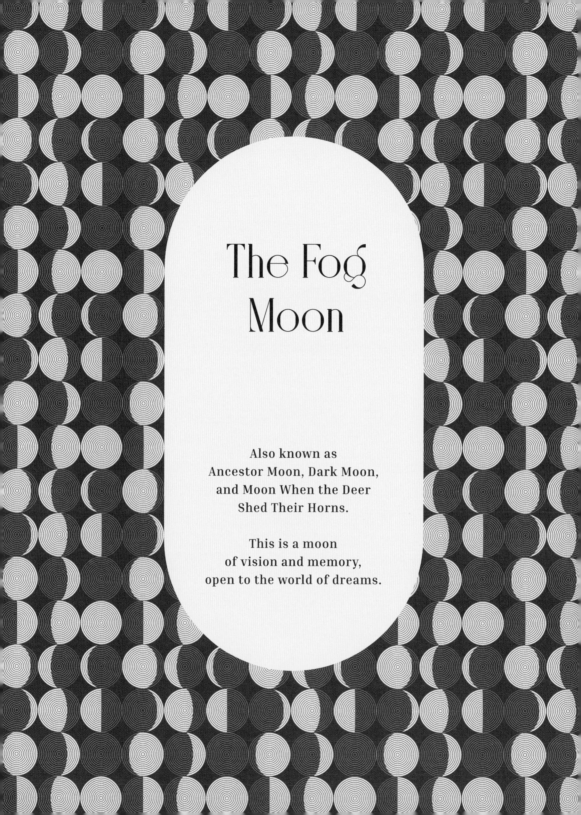

The Fog Moon

Also known as
Ancestor Moon, Dark Moon,
and Moon When the Deer
Shed Their Horns.

This is a moon
of vision and memory,
open to the world of dreams.

W ith the moon of November, we enter a time of rest, immersing ourselves more fully in an inner space that the end of October predicted. This dreamlike world is quiet and sometimes still; but if we look closely, we will find that it is full of transformation.

The November moon is the moment of Scorpio, the zodiac sign most devoted to research and knowledge that has been acquired with no shortcuts, but rather by facing downfall, death, and necessary transformation.

In this period, it becomes easier to connect with the invisible, because life is underground and hidden now. The leaves that fell in October are at the base of the trees now, and they are decomposing in the rain, losing their identity, and becoming food for new life and a promise for the future.

The November moon is a dream moon. The Fog Moon shadows the visible and brings the invisible into focus, and, with the strength of Scorpio, it leads us to explore mystery and magic.

This month is associated with the dark face of Hecate, the tripleform goddess of many cultures. The goddess of crossroads, ravens, and the dead, she whispers to us that it is vital to let some parts of us die so that new visions can come to life. November was the first month of the year for the Celts, almost as if to say that it is in the end that the beginning takes shape, as an idea and as a dream.

The November moon provides the inspiration for facing death, an uncomfortable phenomenon that is almost taboo in Western society when, instead, it is a moment of natural passage wherever there is life. The reflection on death that this month brings is of an organic death that heralds rebirth, a transformative, almost initiatory experience that marks a passage of growth. The year is drawing to an end, and we celebrate that end during this moon, before the regeneration that will occur in December with the sign of Sagittarius. Now we are in the time of the dream where we are allowed to observe, stay, learn, listen, and let the transformation occur.

lunar Phases

WITH THE NEW MOON in November, try the powers of divination using water. Fill a container with water, then light a candle and put it nearby, making sure that its flame is not reflected in the water; the only light in the room must be the light of the candle. Let the shadows and light that appear on the water's surface bring you visions and inspiration. This technique is called "scrying," and this month is the ideal time to practice it.

DURING THE WAXING MOON in November, focus on your transformative processes. How do you feel about the things you let go of last month? Were the cuts you made truly significant? How can you keep with your changes and allow yourself to flow? Make a mood board with photos, illustrations, signs, and anything that inspires you.

WITH THE FULL MOON in November, live, claim your space and make it sacred. This is a good time to stop and listen, to refrain from being active but to remain connected to your inner self. Try to relax, to simply be and to daydream. Think about everything that makes you more flexible and more compliant, and about what you need to truly let go. This could be a good time to practice forgiveness, toward yourself and others.

DURING THE WANING MOON in November, continue the activities you started with the Full Moon, and remember to rest. Examine closely the things you want to know and reveal their mysteries; and as you do, follow the symbols and dreams that can guide you and inspire you. Try to put the suggestions indicated in your dreams at night into practice in your daily life.

Plant

The cypress reminds me of a green flame that points to the sun with its roots firmly in the ground. A sacred tree in many cultures, it is the guardian of the doorstep and it is traditionally planted in cemeteries because of its tendency to develop roots that grow deep rather than horizontally. The roots of the cypress tree are explorers of all that lives underground, in the depths, just like the message of this moon.

The fruit of the cypress, which looks like small pinecones, varies in tone from green to gold, almost as if to indicate an intrinsic sacredness in the plant. The plant's essential oils are contained in its fruit and leaves, which are more like needles than blades.

The cypress is compact and simple. It is associated with Saturn, the planet and the god of contraction, of the return to simplicity, of the heart of things, and of all that which is not useless or superfluous. The shape of the cypress brings to mind that what is important is in what is not visible, like the bones in the body's interior that only become visible upon death.

In many ancient cultures, it was the symbol of resurrection and the seed of rebirth, and, because it was evergreen, the symbol of immortality. Its slow but inexorable growth led to the belief that the cypress tree accompanied the souls of the defunct on their voyage to the next world.

In phytotherapy, the cypress's vasoconstrictive effects make it a useful tool when containment and contraction need to be regulated, just as Saturn teaches us. In aromatherapy, cypress helps us re-emerge from difficult situations caused by a major loss or great transformation.

The message of the cypress is: "Death is only a passage, and life is made of many thresholds."

Cypress

Cupressus L.

XI

125

XI

126

Symbols

MUSHROOMS

Mushrooms belong to the realm of vegetables, but they are a world apart. They love humidity and water, and they have the ability to transform matter.

UNDERGROWTH

This moon leads us into the undergrowth, into contact with the ground, moss, and roots of the plants that grow where the light is weak, where darkness emerges. There is life here, too.

CROSSROADS

A symbol of Hecate, a four-way crossroads has always been considered a place of magic and enchantment where apparitions, ghosts, visions, and legends reveal themselves.

FOG

It is this moon's aquatic form. It lives in suspended waters and blurs the borders of reality.

DEATH

Death, the Tarot card associated with this month is card number XIII, meaning that it is not the final card and that in reality it does not indicate a true end, but only a passage, a threshold to cross, renewal, and the rebirth to new life in which old habits are abandoned.

THE OTHER WORLD

The world we access through our dreams, our sensitive perceptions, and our intuition is a magical space for exchanging energies, memories, and symbols themselves.

PROPHECY

This moon connects with subtle sensations and divination, allowing us to perceive the voices of our ancestors as they convey their messages using symbols we see in our daily life or in our nightly dreams.

Practices and Rituals

Celebrate the end of something, whether it be a relationship, job, or place where you no longer live. Create a ritual to say goodbye and to bless its ending.

Take a walk in a monumental cemetery and choose the headstone that inspires you the most. As you walk in this sacred space, observe and be still.

Create a small altar with the photos of your ancestors, and bring them a small offering of flowers, leaves, or something they loved in life.

Ask a friend who is an expert in mushrooms to take you for a walk in the woods. Mushroom hunters are often reluctant to reveal their favorite spots, but under the supervision of an expert, you just might find some edible mushrooms.

Light a black candle and, as it burns, close those things within you that need to be closed.

Gather a handful of cypress cones and thread them onto a red string to make a necklace to protect your home.

Watch a horror movie with a friend who loves them, and cover your eyes when you need to.

Make a list of your hopes and dreams for the coming year. Start to imagine this new beginning.

Get a deck of Tarot cards and pick one card from the deck for each day of the month, from this November until next October. Even if you do not know how to interpret the oracle, write down what you see in the card in a notebook. It will become your map of inspirations for the year to come.

Dig your hands into dark, soft dirt and ground yourself. You're here, right now: celebrate life.

XI

129

Erykah Badu

Track: "On & On" (from the album *Baduizm*, 1997)

XI

130

Pop Icon

Many music critics have described Erykah Badu as a mysticist. Her music and her art, combined with her political commitment, transmit vibrant emotions; and in her legendary outfits and her high hair turbans, she has the air of an atavistic priestess.

Erykah Badu is an American singer/songwriter who has been defined as the queen of Neo-soul. She is one of the leading artists of the movement. The word *conscious* has been used to describe her music, which reverberates with important social and political observations.

She chose her stage name, Badu, because of her favorite jazz riff, badoo, but she later found out that *badu* in Arabic means "light and truth." This artist connects to the November moon with her shamanic, spiritual character and the authentic, engaged way she presents herself.

Erykah offered a political reflection about death with the music video *Window Seat*, which was filmed in streets around the square where John F. Kennedy was assassinated. In the video, she walks around the square, taking off all her clothes before falling to the ground, shot by an assassin. The video represents her views on how easy it is to hate and kill someone or something you know nothing about.

From Erykah and from the November moon you can learn how important it is to live your life spiritually, and that spirituality is not limited to something immaterial. You can transform it into political, artistic, and communicative action.

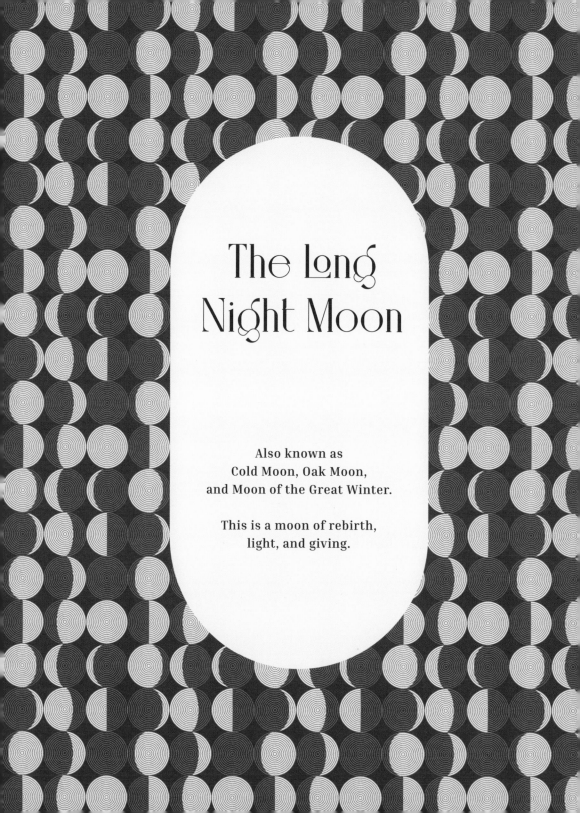

The Long Night Moon

Also known as
Cold Moon, Oak Moon,
and Moon of the Great Winter.

This is a moon of rebirth,
light, and giving.

T he December moon is steeped in the atmosphere of the winter solstice, a symbol of the rebirth of light in the darkest time of the year. December nights, the longest of the year, start to grow shorter after December 21, when we start to perceive the light as it returns. This moon brings an air of renewal and rebirth.

The moon in December is a moment to devote to all the things we want to grow, just as the light begins to grow after a long period of darkness. It is the time of year when we can dedicate ourselves to celebrating and engage with the days of Christmas with a new spirit. We can go beyond the consumeristic aspect that Christmas has taken on in recent years and choose to connect with the message of this moon, living the darkest moment of the year with the hopes of growing light.

In pagan tradition, one of the symbols of rebirth is the tree, particularly the evergreen tree that is so characteristic of this season. Pine and holly, symbols of the month of December, remind us that it is important to resist despite the darkness, to keep believing in the light, and to have faith.

With the moon in December, we can live the beauty of giving. In the darkest hours, giving gifts to our loved ones connects us to them, making us feel that we are not alone and that the light is coming again, to awaken us and begin a new cycle. Think about the beauty of giving, about gratitude, and about the relationship between them. The moon in December takes our hand and leads us on this voyage. Lighting a fire, lighting up a room with candles, and putting decorative lights around your windows are not frivolous gestures; they represent what light, presence, and giving mean to us.

During this period, we can finish projects that we worked on over the year and create space for the things we want to do in the year to come. Stop and evaluate your accomplishments in the previous months, and focus on your desires.

Lunar Phases

WITH THE NEW MOON in December, take stock of the twelve months that are ending. Write down what you accomplished, the areas of your life where you encountered the most difficulties, and the projects you finished. Think about what you learned each month. In general, during this New Moon, let go of the year that is coming to an end and prepare yourself for renewal.

DURING THE WAXING MOON in December, take the time to think about which areas of your life you want to illuminate. Where do you need more light? What aspects need more attention? Use the energy of the Waxing Moon to focus on your intentions for the coming year and have faith in your potential. Think of your future projects as little seeds. What do they need to grow? What color will their flowers be? What will their fruit taste like?

WITH THE FULL MOON in December, celebrate what you have finished during the whole year. What do you want to celebrate from this year that is about to end? When we reach one goal, we often move on to the next without stopping to honor our accomplishment. In this Full Moon, grant yourself something that embodies your concept of festivity—a dinner, bouquet of flowers, or spa day.

DURING THE WANING MOON in December, renew and purify your intentions, environment, and person. Take time to treat yourself, put order back into your spaces, and throw away what is no longer necessary. Use the time of this moon to make gifts and be grateful for reciprocation and everything you have. Use magazine cuttings to make a collage that visually represents what your new year will be.

Plant

olly is the plant associated with this moon, for a number of reasons. The first and most evident is its search for light, despite being a plant that grows in shady locations. Holly is polymorphic; the leaves at its base, where there is little light, are thorny and twisted to protect them from the animals that might eat them, while the leaves that receive more light are more open and have fewer thorns. Dr. Edward Bach chose holly as a floral remedy because of its ability to re-equilibrate anger, rancor, and hate.

Holly is also able to change darkness into light, which is why it has traditionally been considered a resistant plant that brings good luck. At this time of the year in Ancient Rome, it was customary to cut a bundle of holly branches to take indoors as a talisman and then remove it on the twelfth night, the night of the Epiphany. Part of the tradition is still intact today: Epiphany is still the day we traditionally take down Christmas decorations.

For the Celts, the Holly King was the king of the winter months; at the time of the winter solstice, he gave up his scepter to the Oak King, who governed the months of more luxuriant growth. It is said that if you go around a holly plant three times in one direction and then seven times in the other, you will meet the person you will marry. The red berries of the plant are well liked by birds but are toxic for humans. They are a symbol of the sun, whose return they celebrate.

The holly plant has fallen into disuse in phytotherapy; it is currently used only as a Bach floral remedy, as previously mentioned.

The message from holly is: "Keep a long-sighted vision; the light is about to arrive."

Holly

Ilex aquifolium L.

XII

137

Symbols

THE HOLLY KING AND THE OAK KING

The two symbolize the two parts of the year that change with the winter solstice. The Holly King in particular is associated with Santa Claus, because tradition has it that he also brought gifts to the children.

MISTLETOE

Together with ivy and holly, mistletoe symbolizes protection, fertility, and new life. The customary kiss under the mistletoe is associated with the plant's symbology of renewal and growth.

JUDGEMENT

The Tarot card associated with this moon is Judgement, the symbol of rebirth and new life, but also of a calling, an inner vocation, that which moves us to begin our work in the world.

GIFTS

The custom of giving little gifts to the ones we care for is a way to celebrate the end of the year and the conclusion of a cycle, and to wish them wealth and well-being.

THE HEARTH

The hearth is one of the symbols of this time of year. It was customary to light a fire in the hearth on the day of the solstice and keep it burning throughout the entire holiday period as a sign of rebirth. The fire was built on the embers of the day before the solstice and then fed constantly. When the fire went out, its ashes were used as fertilizer.

RED AND GREEN

The colors of this moon remind us of holly. The dark green of its shiny leaves and the red of its bright berries symbolize life, resistance, and rebirth.

Practices and Rituals

Make little seed balls and leave them outside, hanging in the trees for the robins.

Make a list of the gifts you would like to receive, like the letter you used to write for Santa Claus. You can even take it to the post office and mail it if you like.

Make your own candles. As well as being very simple, it is good for practicing meditation in movement. Melt the wax and add essential oils, pour the mixture into a small container, add a wick, and let it solidify. Use your candles to illuminate the darkest days of the year.

Honor simplicity. Feeling stressed by the holidays and the social expectations they bring is normal in this period. Keep to simplicity and let go of perfectionism. Find the time for healthy decompression.

Cook something you like and use your every gesture to infuse it with love, and then give it to the one you love.

Make some mulled wine for your friends and spend the evening together surrounded by chatter and affection.

On the night of the solstice, light a candle to invoke the light that is growing.

Make a playlist full of winter songs and share it on your social network page—share the magic of the solstice!

Make a talisman for the December moon using a sachet of red fabric. Fill it with cinnamon, star anise, and cloves; the warm spices will keep you company on the longest night of the year.

Make a wish like you used to do when you were a child.

Believe in yourself and in your light.

The Blue
Moon

Also known as
the Thirteenth Moon.

This is a moon
of spirituality, love,
and inspiration.

The Blue Moon is a very special moon, a very particular event that can be calculated in two ways. It is *seasonal* if a Full Moon occurs four times in one season, in which case the third Full Moon is the Blue Moon; or it is *calendrical* if the Full Moon occurs twice in the same month, in which case the second moon is the Blue Moon.

The name of the Blue Moon was coined quite recently, in 1946, unlike the names of the other moons we have talked about until now, whose names derive from age-old Anglo-Saxon or Germanic traditions, or from Native American history. In its March 1946 edition, the *Sky and Telescope* magazine published a piece by James Huge Pruett entitled "Once in a Blue Moon." In it, Pruett cited an article that had been recently published in the *Farmer's Almanac*. The article failed to give an accurate interpretation of the Blue Moon, but it suggested the name that would stick with the special moon over the years.

Thanks to its rarity, the Blue Moon is particularly powerful. As with every Full Moon, lunar energy is at its peak, an ideal time to commemorate our successes, celebrate, and work toward making our wishes come true. The Blue Moon adds to the magic of the Full Moon and is truly a special occasion.

Since its occurrence is irregular, its phases are the same as the moon of the month in which it falls. For example, if a Blue Moon occurs as the second Full Moon in the month of November, its phases (Crescent, Waning, and New) will be the same as the moon of this month, the Fog Moon.

Rituals for the Blue Moon

Prepare your sacred place by purifying the air with incense or a Palo Santo stick. Put your place in order and create a quiet space. Light a candle and breathe deeply. Take a piece of paper and write a list of wishes that seem impossible to you now. Write this list in one continuous session, and try to list as many wishes as you can.

When you write them down, try to keep an open heart and positive intentions. Once your list is written, read it aloud to the Blue Moon. Find a way to thank the Triple Goddess, perhaps with a song, dance, or prayer.

Put your list of wishes in a sachet of blue fabric and put it under the moon's rays overnight. In the morning, bring it into the house and put it in a place that is dear to you. Wait and see what happens.

The Blue Moon embodies all three aspects of the Triple Goddess from pagan tradition: the virgin, the mother, and the crone; so it has the ability to connect us to the divine and the spiritual. It can be interesting to use your time during this moon to work on something you believe is unreachable or impossible. Anything can happen once in a Blue Moon!

Use this moon's energy to unblock creative situations in which you are at an impasse, to give yourself a second chance, or to make a spiritual connection to the nature that surrounds you.

Plant

The scientific name for mugwort, *Artemisia vulgaris*, is the first of the plant's close ties to this moon. In fact, the name comes from Artemis, the goddess of the woods and the indomitable spirit.

Another unequivocal sign that mugwort is a lunar plant can be seen in its leaves. Just look at their underside to see the silver color that strongly resembles that of the rays of the Full Moon. The wild spirit of Artemis that walks in the woods alone under the light of the moon, connected to nature, is the soul of this plant.

Its scent will carry you to timeless faraway places like those in your dreams. Mugwort has been associated with travel since ancient times; it is said to protect adventurers. Put a mugwort leaf in your suitcase to avoid losing it and travel with a branch of mugwort in your car to protect your journeys. It is a prophetic plant that is used to favor dreaming.

It has a regulatory effect on the menstrual cycle; it favors fertility, and during menopause it helps prevent osteoporosis. Mugwort picked during the Full Moon can be used to make an excellent oil that can also be used to relieve menstrual cramps or for body massage. To prepare a vinegar rich in vitamins B, C, and A, calcium, potassium, and iron, put a few handfuls of mugwort leaves in a bottle of wine vinegar and let them macerate for three weeks.

Artemis lives between worlds, and meeting her means that you must examine your visions and your dreams more closely. Pick a small branch of mugwort and put it under your pillow. In the morning, write your dreams in a notebook, including the colors and sensations you experienced.

The message from mugwort is: "Keep your eyes open, especially when you dream."

Mugwort

Artemisia vulgaris

XIII

147

XIII

148

Symbols

STARS

Stars represent wishes and hopes. They are associated with this exceptional moon because, like this moon, they represent something that seems impossible but that might happen under a lucky star or a shooting star.

AMETHYST

A symbol of balance and of the union between opposites, amethyst is associated with this moon for its ability to bring dreams and facilitate daydreams. It also protects travel and travelers as well as the spiritual voyage of each one of us.

BLUE

Blue is the color associated with this moon, even if the moon itself is not actually blue. Celebrate the moon by dressing in blue, buying blue flowers, or practicing anything that brings blue into your life.

UNICORN

A pure and magical animal, the unicorn is a horse with a horn and wings. To see one is a rare and lucky event. According to Jung's analytical psychology, the unicorn represents the union between opposites and therefore balance and harmony. It is both strength and unity.

THE FOOL

The Tarot card associated with this moon is the one with no number. It represents unpredictability, discovery, originality, and the ability to believe in what we hope will happen, just because we believe. The Fool is unique, just like the Blue Moon. It is the beginning and the end, the adventure into an unknown fantasy world. The card also represents purity and innocence.

Practices and Rituals

Go out and bask in the light of the Blue Moon; bathe in the light of its rays. If it falls in one of the warm months, do it naked in a protected location.

Listen to the sound of the Tibetan bells or something similar, to connect to the power of the moon.

Do something you have wanted to do for some time but that you have not done yet. It can be cooking a new dish, seeing a movie that intrigues you, taking a new way home from work, or taking pictures at sunset.

Look for a guided lunar meditation and take the time to do it today. There are many to be found online.

Create a sacred space using the color blue: candles, fabric, food, crystals, lights, and clothes. Connect with the color.

Make a tisane with blueberries and mallow; put them in a cup of lukewarm water and put it under the rays of the Blue Moon overnight. In the morning, you will find a light-blue tisane full of lunar energy.

Even if you do not know how to paint, take a big piece of paper and some watercolors and liberate your creativity on this magical night.

Think about the diversity, originality, and individuality of each of us.

Put blue food coloring in your bathwater. As you immerse yourself in the tub, envision a blue light that is taking the weariness, the negativity, and the difficulties away from your life and giving you brightness and focus.

Put a blue ribbon in your hair or in your pocket, and keep it there all day as a secret message between you and the moon.

Janis Joplin

Track: "Kozmic Blues" (from the album *I Got Dem Ol' Kozmic Blues Again Mama!*, 1969)

Pop Icon

Janis was unique. Her voice was unique, her lifestyle was unique, and the emotions her voice still conveys are unique. She could only have been a singer. When you have a true vocation, you carry it inside you like a shiny jewel.

Her life was incredibly short, and it seems impossible that at just twenty-seven, she was able to revolutionize notes and singing, and music itself. She is the embodiment of her era, the era of hippies and the peaceful revolution of the flower children. Her style was original and unique, just like she was, and that is her connection to this moon; a rare moon that almost never occurs on the same day of the year and that you may have to wait years to see again. It takes its time and cares nothing about being the odd one.

Besides having an incredible voice, Janis had the strength to convey emotions that were vibrant, heartbreaking, and dramatic, and, at the same time, full of life. She was the priestess of feelings and in some ways it was those emotions that drowned her, moved her, and led her astray. The life she sang about was still beautiful and vibrant—full of joy, rage, and fear, but never the fear of *feeling*; the Blue Moon, with its spiritual message and its connection to both sentimental and universal love, teaches us that we should not fear our emotions either.

"On stage I make love to twenty-five thousand people," she said. The Blue Moon inspires us to love without the fear of loving fully and to feel all the love there is in your every cell, even when you are sad and feel like no one loves you. Look up to the sky and look at the moon, and remember, you are made of that same light.

Lunar Calendar

You can use this special lunar calendar to record the lunar phases and your moods. Beneath the calendar is a legend with symbols you can use to indicate the New Moon, First Quarter, Full Moon, and Last Quarter in each month of the year.

You can record the days in which these moon phases occur, starting from the month you purchase this book or from the one in which you start using it. If you want, you can also take note of how you feel that day, in that particular phase of the moon: your feelings and your emotions, using emoticons or other symbols that your imagination suggests.

Remember to use a pencil so you can erase and start your lunar calendar all over again!

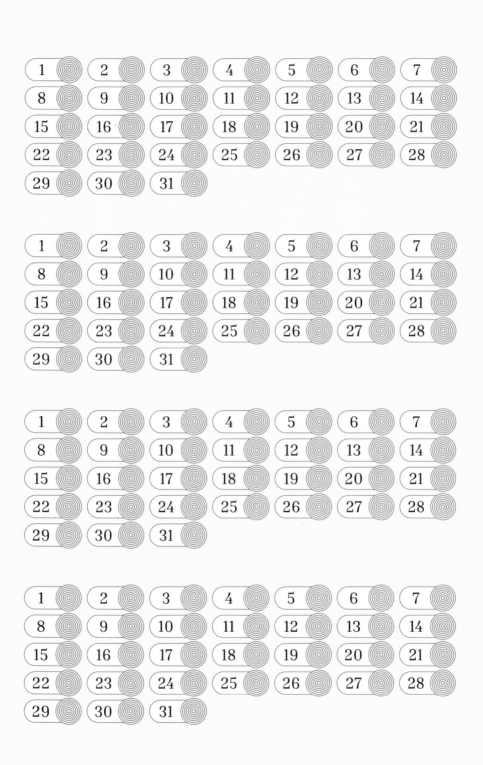

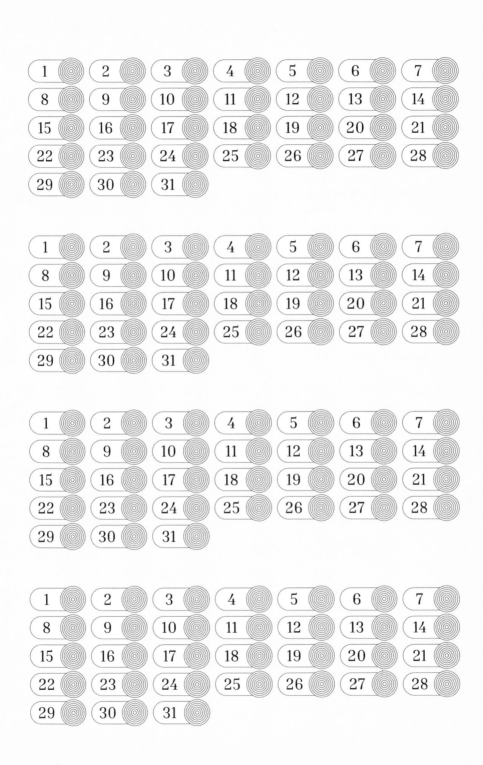

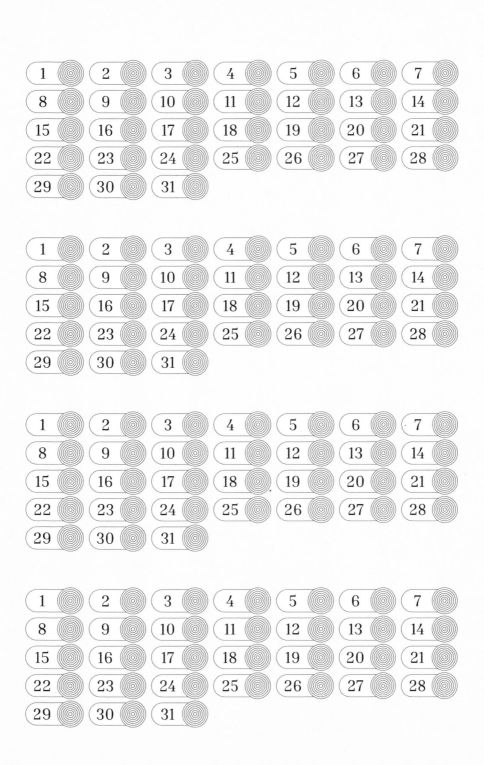

Bibliography

Berger, Judith. *Herbal Rituals.* Smashwords, Pacific Grove, CA, 1998.

Cattabiani, Alfredo. *Lunario. Dodici mesi di miti, feste, leggende e tradizioni popolari d'Italia.* Mondadori, Milano, IT, 2002.

———. *Florario. Miti leggende e simboli di fiori e piante.* Mondadori, Milano, IT, 1996.

Cunningham, S. *Cunningham's Encyclopedia of Magical Herbs.* Llewellyn Worldwide, Portland, OR, 1985.

Mecozzi, Karin. *Ars herbaria. Piante medicinali nel respiro dell'anno.* Natura e Cultura editrice, Alassio, IT, 2012.

Morrison, Dorothy. *The Craft: A Witch's Book of Shadows.* Llewellyn Worldwide, Portland, OR, 2001.

Patterson, Rachel. *Moon Magic.* Moon Books, New Alresford, UK, 2014.

Roux, Jessica. *Floriography. An Illustrated Guide to the Victorian Language of Flowers.* Andrews McMeel, Kansas City, MO, 2020.

Toll, Maia. *The Illustrated Herbiary. Guidance and Rituals from 36 Bewitching Botanicals.* Storey, North Adams, MA, 2018.

Online References

www.actaplantarum.org
www.cavernacosmica.com
www.enciclopediadelledonne.it
www.ilcerchiodellaluna.it
www.thepeculiarbrunette.com
www.wortsandcunning.com

Acknowledgments

This book would not exist if many of the people dear to me had not charted the course that made it possible. I would like to thank Francesca Matteoni, writer, friend, and companion on many adventures; she opened the way for me to reach my goal. I also thank Balthazar Pagani, whose visions often coincide with mine and whose imagination is a precious resource. I want to thank my moon sisters: Silvia, Virginia, Serena, Giulia, Onda, Linda, Lucia, Alessia, Eleonora, Emanuela, Nina, Alice, Doriana, Valentina, Anna, Gabriella—each of you is a moon goddess and holds a piece of my heart. Thanks to my mother, Angela, who wrote and mapped the worlds—I know she watches over me, hidden in the light of the moon; and to my grandmothers who taught me my love of plants and the magic of daily life. Thanks to Gabriele, who stands beside me and is so special that maybe he comes from the moon. Thanks to my beloved animals Bambi, Cipolla, and Mirtillo who live on this earth with me, and Hero and Eva who protect me from somewhere near the end of the rainbow. Thanks to all the friends I have not named but that I carry in my heart, including those who have left us because they will always be a part of my story and of the illuminated path that, every day, keeps me believing in the sensitive, in the imaginary, and in inclusive love. Above all, I want to thank all the children who love to read, because maybe one day they will write new dreams and new worlds.

C. L.

CECILIA LATTARI is an herbalist who earned her degree from the University of Bologna and a professional actress who graduated from the Bologna School of Theater. She is a socio-pedagogist involved in sensory- and imagination-based education with the use of a variety of languages including writing, theater, the connection to the natural world, and helping relationships. She works in the field of relationships, stimulating the connection between people and their most authentic parts, using theater and the sensory experience with the plant world.

She lives in a small town in the Apennine Mountains in Tuscany, near the woods. The moon's light shines on her door, and often she has long dialogues with the moon and with her cats.

EMILIO IGNOZZA is a graphic artist who lives in Milan. He has a degree in architecture, even though he has never practiced. Geometry, modules, and patterns have always played a key role in his approach to design.

Thanks to both technical and humanistic studies, he became passionate about art, design, and visual communications.

His interests include illustration, photography, and typographic design.

He has been a part of *the*World*of*DOT studio since 2012, where his specialty is editorial graphics. He has created projects for covers and series for a number of Italian publishers.